Seeing God's Beauty from Ashes

Barbara J. Cornelius

Wheredepony
Press

ACKNOWLEDGEMENTS

I have everlasting gratitude for my Lord and Savior rescuing me from the finality of death and giving me eternal life with Him. His gift of salvation has highlighted my life on earth in ways that have brought me joy in the victories and comfort in the trials and losses. Experiencing His love throughout my days has given me the wonderful anticipation of going home to live in His presence in heaven. Thank you, Father.

I am also extremely grateful for the man He brought into my life to be my husband for almost fifty-seven years. Larry was much more than just the love of my life. He made my life complete. His heart for me was a gift I will always cherish. My days with him were full of personal growth, joy, and love. We fought together, laughed together, and together we grew in our relationship with the Lord. Any strife that came between us was simply covered by the deep enduring love we had for each other. All the days of our marriage were treasured by us because we truly became one. Although Larry is no longer on earth with me, I will love him throughout eternity. Thank you, Father for loaning him to me.

Table of Contents

Isaiah 43:2

"When you pass through the waters, I will be with you: and through the rivers, they shall not overwhelm you; when you walk through fire you shall not be burned, and the flame shall not consume you."

Isaiah 61:3

"He will give you a crown of beauty instead of ashes, the oil of joy instead of mourning and a garment of praise instead of a spirit of despair."

Psalm 139:15-16

"My frame was not hidden from you, when I was being made in secret, intricately woven in the depths of the earth. Your eyes saw my unformed substance; in your book were written, every one of them, the days that were formed for me, when as yet there was none of them."

Seeing God's Beauty from Ashes

Introduction

Iam in the twilight years of my life, and when I look in the mirror, I definitely see a lady in her seventies. Yet, I still feel young in many ways. I have a few close friends who, like me, say, "I am twelve years old *inside*." I even have a former student who is now about fifty years old, say when he sees me, "We're still both twelve!" Of course, our bodies may disagree with this assessment, but our minds still have the capacity to look at the present with much curiosity, joy, and anticipation of a bright future.

I met my husband when I was eighteen and he was twenty, and we had almost sixty years together, with fifty-seven of them married. Where did all of that time go? You observe that the years are going by quickly. You see your babies quickly become toddlers, then teenagers, and all too soon they are adults with their own children. Yes, time just flies by. Looking back at all the years I had with my husband, it should feel like a very long time. It doesn't. Because he is no longer with me, it seems like our time together ended in the "blink of an eye."

I have had a very rich life, and I have an unending appreciation for all the love my family and friends have given me. A loving husband, two children and their spouses, and eight grandchildren are most certainly gifts of prosperity from God. I feel certain when I transition from living on this side of eternity, I will arrive at a beautiful, everlasting place which God has reserved for me. It is there that I believe I will be fully alive for the first time ever! I envision myself in heaven, relieved of all my burdens, living an abundant life and being able to joyfully sit at the feet of Jesus. I can't wait.

The number of days, hours, minutes, and seconds left to me is known only by God, and I appreciate that lack of information. Being fully aware of the exact timing of my "heavenly promotion" might diminish my ability to focus on the present and tempt me to just anticipate the joy that awaits me in heaven. I don't want to squander the time left to me. I want to savor today's precious moments with my family and friends, and fulfill my purpose here on earth.

Of course, I don't have a choice about knowing my "due date", and in the meantime I look forward to the new beginnings that await me in each of my earthly tomorrows! I don't experience them alone. The Lord is all around me wherever I am, and I feel His presence. Sometimes, when I am gifted with moments of laughter, I suspect He is there right beside me, laughing. With all of my goofiness, I provide lots of material for us to laugh together. I relish those times.

My heavenly Father could clearly see the words written on each page of my life's story long, long before I was even conceived. He knew that sorrows, times of devastation, and tremendous victories would be there. He saw, even before I took my first breath, how all of them would be woven together according to the plan He had for me.

Just like a forest fire produces ashes which release nutrients in the soil to promote new growth, God took my "ashes" to not only enrich my life, but also the lives of others. He transformed many of my agonizing experiences into a source of spiritual wealth that I would have never asked for, but treasure deeply. It is in those times of darkness that I felt myself drawing ever closer to Him, the Living God of the universe. His investment of love in me is immeasurable, and I marvel that He thought I was worth sacrificing His only Son in order to save me. He created an individual niche for me in the universe, and it cannot be inhabited by anyone else. We are so special to God, that He does this for each of us.

Savoring all that I am, He walks beside me as the pages of my life are being freshly written every day. He protects me by guiding every step and detail of my earthly journey. When I occasionally take a treacherous detour, He leads me back to safety. He has given all that He has to empower me to have a victorious life. I want more than anything for Him to be proud of me. After all, He is my Father.

After my last breath is taken and my life story finished, I will not cease to exist. God authors my book of life, and it will someday rest in His *personal library* along with those of other saints. I will always have a reserved place in the universe. God made this provision for me, and I live every day in gratitude for this. I so look forward to expressing my thankfulness to Him when I see Him face to face.

Most of us on this side of eternity have endured many heartbreaking moments, but God's Word insures us that when we go home to be with Him, there will be no more tears. Our burdens will no longer exist. He will replace *all* of our "ashes" with beauty. God sees how all of the trials we are enduring today are important to the tapestry of our lives and to the fabric of others' lives. Nothing we experience will be useless to Him. Not one day of our lives is wasted in His eyes.

The pages written in my life story will never be erased. Your pages will not be erased when you take *your* last breath. Our Father savors them too much to allow that to ever happen. Victories, some of which were experienced on "mountain tops" and some which happened in dark valleys, are remembered there. They are embedded in our spirits and souls which flourish spectacularly when we go home to our Lord.

Read God's Word each and every day, and you will see that since before time began, He has been the author of all the stories in the universe. He chose to include mine. He chose to include yours. You are so cherished by Him that He thinks about you all the time, even as you read the words on this page. I matter to Him. You matter to Him. Praise Him. Praise Him. He is so worthy.

The fire poppy uses heat, smoke or charred soil as signals to sprout. Without the fire, they would not sprout. Perhaps, they give us a beautiful example of God making beauty from ashes.

Barbara J. Cornelius

Isaiah 61:1-3

"The Spirit of the Sovereign Lord is on me, because the Lord has anointed me to preach good news to the poor. He has sent me to bind up the brokenhearted, to proclaim freedom for the captives, and release from darkness for the prisoners, to proclaim the year of the Lord's favor and the day of vengeance of our God, to comfort all who mourn, and provide for those who grieve in Zion-to bestow on them a crown of beauty instead of ashes, the oil of gladness instead of mourning, and a garment of praise instead of a spirit of despair.

Chapter One

God's Beauty from the Ashes of a Car

One day I was shocked when my nineteen-year-old grandson frantically rang our doorbell. Just as he had driven up to the circular driveway in front of our house, he saw flames coming from under the hood of his car. When I opened the front door, he blurted out, "My car is on fire! Do you have a fire extinguisher?"

By the time I had desperately conducted a quick, fruitless search for an extinguisher, the car was engulfed in flames. Our neighbor who lived directly across the street was home to see our plight, and he came running over with his, but it was much too late to do any good. I had already called the fire department, and now all my husband, grandson, and I could do was watch helplessly as the flames came closer and closer to our house. By the time we heard the sirens announcing the arrival of our volunteer fire department, the flames were within three feet of destroying our home.

As I stood in the yard and witnessed the impending disaster, I felt supernatural calm and peace that defied what I was seeing. The silent, prayerful conversation I was having with my Heavenly Father was guiding my emotions and building a hedge of protection against fear. I calmly thought about the possibility of losing everything in the house.

Several of our neighbors came to see what was creating so much commotion. We hadn't seen many of them in several weeks, and their light conversation, devoid of any panic in the midst of our trauma, was welcomed. Finally, the huge amount of water sprayed from the hoses of the firetruck quenched the flames, and victory was proclaimed. Our home survived, totally untouched by the fire.

Seeing all this unfold, a memory from a few years ago came flooding into my mind. A couple in our church had suffered the sudden destruction of their home and everything in it. It had burned to the ground while they were out of the country. The testimony they gave a few weeks after returning home to the devastation was resonating in my thoughts. After taking inventory of everything lost, they had tearfully come to the realization of which items were replaceable and which ones were not because of sentimental value. They then shared with many others that they would not mourn over their situation. What was most precious to them was not material things, it was their faith walk with God and they trusted Him in all circumstances. Many people in our church were very inspired by their response and came to their rescue in any way they could. Their loss became a gain for many of us. It strengthened our walk with the Lord.

What remained from this latest battle was the shell of the car, the empty wheels where the rubber tires had liquified, and thousands of pieces of glass scattered all over the blackened driveway. My grandson's university books, homework papers, and some clothing items were also ruined. He told me later that the Bible, I had proudly given him a few years ago with his name printed in gold, was in the fused glove compartment. I had written a personal inscription in the front of it, and I had hoped he would keep it for many, many years. This gift was a reminder to him of how important faith was to his grandmother, and that was my true legacy for him.

Even though the Bible could not be retrieved and was lost to him, I felt that perhaps something more valuable was given. God's Word being sealed off in the midst of this trauma was a message. I believed it was a sign of God's protection for Brandon's safety. God was gifting us with a spiritual landmark that will be shared for many generations in our family. When the flames of devastation threaten, God is there with us.

God's protection was also clearly seen in the location of the fire. The fire might have claimed Brandon's life had it happened under different circumstances. The outcome might have been horrendous had his car caught fire while he was driving on the interstate! His car burning up while safely parked in our driveway was a blessing we claimed. God was going out of His way to teach us about beauty in the midst of ashes.

Brandon tearfully asked me on that day, "Did I do anything wrong to cause this?" He was inexperienced at car maintenance and felt instinctively he had possibly been lax and overlooked something important. My husband and I, knowing the history and age of his car, assured him that was not the case. It was a malfunction of the electrical system, and not Brandon's fault. I promised Brandon that not only had he not caused this disaster, but that someday God would transform the ordeal into something very valuable for him. Grace given to us and Brandon on that day was gratefully received.

I recently heard a beautiful devotional given by a friend of mine who spoke about the ashes of her life. She saw them as opportunities for God to turn them into something beautiful. She used as an analogy what happens to the soil in the aftermath of a forest fire. Dead trees and decaying plant matter are there in the midst of the devastation, but that is not the end of the story.

The chemical changes resulting from the fire, along with increased soil temperatures, stimulate microbial activity. This increased activity results in higher rates of decomposition, and the release of readily available nutrients into the soil. The ashes return nutrients to the soil instead of keeping them captive in old vegetation. The analogy is a striking reminder that as we go through the fire of our own life's trials, God releases strengths inside of us that were not realized beforehand. Wow!

Job in the Old Testament could tell us much about how God turned his ashes into beauty. He surmised that before his gut-wrenching suffering, he had just heard about God. Now, because of what he went through, he had seen Him first hand (Job 42:5).

Isaiah spoke eloquently about the character of God and gave prophecy about Him taking our ashes and exchanging them for a crown of beauty. Many others in God's Word described how He did this for His people, and many living today can also give confirmation of God doing that in their own lives.

God never intends for us to stay mired in our sin, pain, or deep sorrows. He stores beauty in the future for us every time we walk in a dark valley of despair. We do not walk alone. God is there at our side. He rescues, heals, and transforms us.

Ashes of a fire transformed into a testimony of God's Protection

Brandon at
nineteen
2016

Psalm 18:31-33

For who is God, but the Lord? And who is a rock, except our God- the God who equipped me with strength and made my way blameless. He made my feet like the feet of a deer and set me secure on the heights.

Philippians 4:5-7

Do not be anxious about anything, but in every situation, by prayer and petition with thanksgiving, present your requests to God. And the peace of God, which transcends all understanding, will guard you hearts and minds in Christ Jesus.

Chapter Two

Making Peace with Your Pain

I was amazed to read the words of this young, beautiful woman who lost her left leg in a helicopter crash. Kirstie Ennis had bravely declared "I have learned to make peace with my pain." Her story of courage began in a war zone half way around the world in Afghanistan. In addition to the loss of her leg, she had also experienced severe trauma to her brain, spine, neck, shoulder, and face when the helicopter she was in eleven years ago fell from the sky. She was seventeen when she enlisted, right out of high school, and only twenty-one when she was injured.

On that fateful day, Kirstie was in her second tour with the United States Marine Corps and riding in a CH-53D helicopter. It had been for a routine resupply mission which she had done many times. The last thing she remembered before everything went black was seeing the ground come toward the helicopter. Upon regaining consciousness, she discovered her entire body was riddled with burns and broken bones.

I read about Kirstie's life story in 2019 when she won the Pat Tillman Award for Service at the ESPYs. This award is given in memory of Tillman who put his NFL career with the Arizona Cardinals on hold to serve with the Army Rangers in the aftermath of 9/11. Tillman was tragically killed in Afghanistan in April 2004, and a foundation was set up in his name by friends and family. Kirstie was selected because

13

she exhibited the same drive, courage and desire to push the limits, and achieve her best as Pat Tillman had done in his life.

Now in her early thirties, Kristie has experienced more pain in her life than most of us do in our entire lives. There had been over forty surgeries on her leg before it was amputated. The loss of part of her jaw necessitated her having speech therapy and cognitive therapy was required because her brain injury affected her comprehension. Her beautiful face and slim figure do not reveal the totality of what she has been through. Just looking at her missing limb would not give you the entire story of her courageous journey.

Because of her injuries and constant pain, there was a time that Kristie did not want to live. Her parents were there at her side to encourage her. Her father challenged her with statements like, "You want to finish the work of the enemy?"

An epiphany came upon realizing her life's work was just beginning. Kristie had joined the Marine Corps as a teenager to protect people who can't protect themselves. This spirit of selflessness came to life again with her recognizing the power she had to help others. Lessening their pain, decreased her own.

Even though her recovery is on-going, today Kristie has declared victory, not just for herself, but for others whose lives she has touched. She aspires to continue the path she is on for those who love her, and for those who haven't even met her in person.

The darkest moments of her life have catapulted her into some of the best moments of her life. Kristie has chosen one of the most unlikely hobbies for herself, one that helps her to continue practicing her courage: mountain climbing. Her plan is to climb each of the Seven Summits-the highest peak on each of the seven continents. She dedicates each climb to raising awareness and money for nonprofits that support education, opportunity, and healing in the outdoors.

Less than a year after she started climbing, she took on Mount Kilimanjaro, the highest summit in Africa. Not only did she make it to the top, she used her climb to help raise $150,000 for clean water for the local community.

This beautiful woman was even chosen to be the first female amputee to grace annual Pin-Ups for Vets calendar for 2018. This charity benefits veteran's hospitals in the United States. Kristie wore heels for the first time in the pictures taken, showing a new vision of beauty for women who have lost self-esteem due to physical imperfections from accidents, cancer surgeries, and even birth defects.

She says that an important part of her journey is to embrace failure, because right actions follow right perspectives and this leads to success. She believes that if you put your head and heart in the right place, you can overcome your physical and emotional trials. She encourages others to just rest a moment less when they are striving, and endure a fraction more.

Kristie has made peace with her pain, and on the days when she falters, she reminds herself of those who may be watching. Perhaps it is a young person who needs someone to be a pillar of hope. So many people are looking for some inspiration to keep going. Having walked through a dark, painful valley and with every step taken today, she inspires others to follow her lead. Her courage leaves "footprints" for others to walk in on their way to victory.

To multiply her efforts, she has established the Kristie Ennis Foundation to empower disabled, veteran and minority communities. Kristie believes by building their confidence and enabling them to improve their mobility through therapeutic climbing, they can become more than they ever dreamed. God transformed her "ashes" into an amazing victory which will bless perhaps thousands and thousands of people. Maybe even many more than that.

What pain are you dealing with in your life? Perhaps, it is physical or it is emotional from the trauma you experienced in the past. Present it to the Lord and ask Him to give you the kind of healing that will give you peace. He will take this burden from you and give your life new purpose. He will enable you to live a life that not only brings you fulfillment, but also inspires others to walk in your "footprints." The beauty that comes from your "ashes" will bring much glory to God and His kingdom.

Barbara J. Cornelius

Psalm 91:11-12

For he will command his angels concerning you to guard you in all your ways. On their hands they will bear you up, lest you strike your foot against a stone.

Psalm 139:16

Your eyes saw my unformed body; all the days ordained for me were written in your book before one of them came to be.

Chapter Three
Jennifer's Angels

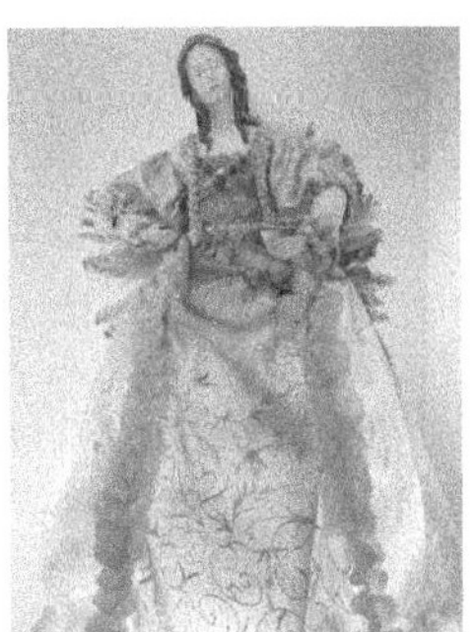

The car suddenly appeared in the darkness heading straight towards my daughter's car. Headlights shining from her car did not deter the impatient driver from passing a slower car ahead of him on the two-lane highway. Jennifer had to quickly swerve over to the side of the road to avoid a head on collision. Miraculously, she did not lose control of her car or land in the ditch next to the road. She had been traveling to the elementary school where she was a teacher. The required early arrival time necessitated she leave in darkness every morning to make the thirty-five- minute trip. Jennifer's angels were at her side when this happened. I feel sure of it. This frightening experience which occurred recently is not the only time Jennifer's life has been in peril.

When she was a baby, I stood at her baby bed every night, fervently praying over her small body. She was the daughter I had prayed for and when she was born, I looked at her beautiful face and dark curly hair and felt total exhilaration! When I entered this world, I was a very fat, bald baby, and so my observation of this gorgeous baby girl was that, thankfully, she had inherited her appearance from others in the family gene pool!

Shortly after I had given birth to her, without the use of any drugs, the attending physician asked me if I wanted to walk back to my room. I gleefully took him up on the offer, and stopped on the way to call my family before passing out. This was a few decades ago, and thankfully I believe this is no longer an option given to "ditzy" mothers like me. On second thought, he might have been asking me in jest and was shocked to see me gingerly hop off the table.

Nightly, when I spoke to my Heavenly Father about my precious infant, I asked him to send His angels to protect her and bring her safely to the next morning's arrival. She was my second baby and unlike my first child, she slept very soundly during the night. As a baby, our son cried frequently throughout the night, and with great weariness my husband or I would gather him up to rock him back to sleep. We were delighted to have him, and concluded sleep deprivation was a very small price to pay for such a wonderful gift!

Having a baby who provided my husband and me a good night's sleep should have been a welcome experience, but my fretful nature crept in. I needed to be reassured every night that God had my beautiful baby girl in His loving Hands, and that He would send his protective angels to her side while she slept.

Frequently, I would read about sudden death syndrome in babies and feared that fate for my child. I knew my baby and I were deeply loved by God, and I was sure that babies and parents who suffered this tragedy were equally loved by Him. I could reconcile all of this only by acknowledging that His ways were ones I could not fathom. His thoughts were not my thoughts. He is God. I am not. Still, I could find peace and retire at night only after my prayers had been offered in the presence of my child. I could then entrust her to my Heavenly Father.

My daughter is now fifty years old (although she doesn't look it), and I believe that someday when she goes home to be with the Lord, she will see the many, many times when God sent His angels to divert her path from tragedy. I know of only a few of her close calls with death, and they reassure me that God's plan is always in place, no matter the circumstances.

Some of Jennifer's life-saving rescues have involved the appearance of deer as she made her way to and from school. One of these happened on her way home several years ago. Right after she had traveled through a major intersection, she was suddenly greeted by a deer in the middle of the highway. The deer was just standing there! She slammed on the brakes to miss him, and fortunately no one was behind her to crash into the back of her car. Amazingly, the deer disappeared into the surroundings untouched.

Another close encounter with a deer occurred after that experience. In the dim light of the early morning hours as she was on her way to school, a large, golden-brown deer suddenly jumped in front of her car. No time to apply the brakes. Knowing she was going to hit him at full speed, she closed her eyes to brace for impact. Nothing happened. No collision. She quickly opened her eyes to see no sign of the deer on the roadside. He was nowhere in sight.

On another occasion, a very inexplicable close call happened a few minutes after she had left school and was driving home. She glanced up at her rearview mirror and saw a car quickly approaching right behind her. It was a clear weather day and the road she was traveling was completely straight with no curves, hills, and no visibility issues. Still, the driver seemed to be oblivious to her presence. She had absolutely nowhere to go to avoid the imminent collision.

Only moments later, she looked again in the rearview mirror to see the oblivious driver's car parked on the side of the road. He had exited his car with his driver's door left wide open, and was seated in the grass with his head placed in his hands. This disheveled young man seemed to be stunned and confused. He appeared to be emotionally distraught, possibly about what he had come so close to experiencing. A collision would have certainly brought an end to his life and that of my daughter's.

I feel certain that Jennifer's heavenly protectors rescued both of them. There was no screeching of tires or any other loud sound to accompany this close call. This stranger was about to collide with my daughter's car, and then he mysteriously appeared in a different location. It is unknown if he was on drugs or diminished by some health problem, but the Hand of God overcame what he was lacking that day.

Jennifer's angels who escorted her to safety in all of these incidents are also at her side in her elementary classroom. She has a divine calling to be a teacher, and her obedience to God's voice has given her great perseverance in the midst of a stressful and demanding occupation. Her talents and teaching abilities began to bloom front and center when she was only thirteen years old and was beginning to baby sit. She was not content to just keep the children entrusted to her safe and out of trouble, and she was determined to *not* use the television as a backup baby sitter. She has been endowed with the gift of being able to communicate God's loving nature to others, and to that cause she entertained children she supervised with a bag full of fun, creative activities.

One recent school year challenged the use of her talents and dedication. If God gives you a calling and you are obedient to that, trials and tests of endurance will definitely follow. However, God is very proud about who you are in Him and He will supply the resources you need to succeed. Jennifer had a unique opportunity to see God do this in a very stressful year of teaching.

Jennifer's assignment was only fourteen fifth grade students, but all of them needed extra support for all the academic subjects. Some of them were on a first-grade reading level, and many had physical and emotional issues which required special compensation for them to be successful.

The week before the first day of school, Jennifer and I partnered to prepare "God's campground" by praying over the entire room. Every student desk and chair were anointed with oil and prayer. All doors, windows, computers, etc. were dedicated to God's work with His children. We asked the Lord to send His angels to preside over all that took place there and to bless every person who came into that space.

All throughout the school year, people would walk into her classroom and comment about the sweet atmosphere they sensed there. Perhaps this was a way that Jennifer's divine messengers were making their presence known. Remarkedly, at the end of the school year, state required testing revealed that the students had accomplished the required academic growth. Moreover, Jennifer received glorious letters from parents describing their children's success. One parent's letter spoke about the great inspiration Jennifer had been to her child, saying, "It was the best school year he had ever had."

My daughter faced physical costs from that year of enormous expectations. She allowed herself only about four hours of sleep a night. She decided she needed all the time she could muster to bring every child's promise to fruition. Exhaustion was her constant companion. I believe God's protectors encouraged her and gave her "eagles wings," so she could finish her assigned mission.

Jennifer has also suffered through some extremely challenging times in her personal life. Her divorce from her first husband left her with a crushed spirit. The Holy Spirit transformed this pain into her heightened awareness and compassion about the emotional distress of others. She had been left with two babies to raise alone, and yet, she also taught school while finishing an advanced degree in education. God was there at her side to guide her through this deep valley, and I believe her angels were also present. Perhaps they sang softly over her so that she could have the strength to be a beacon of light for others.

Six years after her divorce, Jennifer married a Godly man who was an answer to our prayers for a husband that would deeply love her and her children." This union has brought great happiness to our entire family. I lovingly call her husband of eighteen years "Saint Earl." The joy that Jennifer and Earl receive from being together almost came to an end a year after they were married. They were expecting their first child together when the threat of tragedy came into their lives.

My husband and I were out of town when we were told about the emergency situation threatening Jennifer's life. We frantically made our way home, with frequent updates as we traveled. Jennifer had a severe case of pneumonia and had been placed in the intensive care unit at our local hospital. The situation was dire enough that she required a ventilator to assist her breathing. Upon arriving at her bedside, I began praying for her as I had done when she was an infant. My husband, her father, stood next to me as we both cried softly.

Jennifer was mostly unaware of what was happening around her, and the prayers of many, many others were urgently being said to reinforce ours. In an attempt to save her life, the doctors had safely delivered her baby girl six weeks early. Jennifer was at great risk of dying and leaving behind two small children, a tiny baby girl, and her husband. We learned later that the doctors thought she might be only a few hours from death. Looking at CT scans, they determined that her lungs were two-thirds solid with the consistency of cream cheese.

We needed a miracle, and as I pleaded with God for this, I felt that her angels were again at her bedside. Perhaps, they were the ones who had guarded over her as a baby. I am sure that after she triumphantly survived this crisis, these invisible messengers "sang and danced" with me in celebration.

I have prayed with great intensity for other loved ones to be healed and God's answer was, "No, not on this side of eternity." I recently learned about the tragic story of a young woman who had lived close to my daughter's home fifteen years ago. She attended the same church as my daughter and her family.

At the age of thirty this young mother died of pneumonia and left behind two young children and a husband. Many, many prayers had also been offered for her. God's heart-breaking answer to those prayers cannot be understood on this side of eternity. We have no way of knowing why this young woman was not saved so she could have held her first grandson who was born recently. Surely her protectors were there when she died, escorting her to heaven so she could dance with them there.

Still, for my beautiful daughter the answer to our prayers was, "Yes." She and Earl later had a baby boy who was obviously also meant to be here. God made sure of that. My gratitude to God for preserving Jennifer's life is with me every day. It never leaves me, and causes me to always ask for the miraculous healing of others.

It is my belief that my daughter has been kept safe because her life story has not yet been completed. She has known the Lord since she was a small child, and she reaches out with His love to her family, the students in her classrooms, and even strangers. I tell her all the time, "When I grow up, I want to be like you!" (I am in my seventies, so I am running out of time.)

God continually uses her trials to increase the empathy for others she has had since she was a small child. She has comforted many people who have suffered through illnesses, injustices and divorces. I don't believe that anything she has endured has been wasted. Her pain has had a purpose. I see her pouring the intrinsic value of her challenging experiences back into the lives of others. God is definitely touching people through her with His loving Spirit.

We have no explanation why some life stories end early, breaking the hearts of so many. Jesus Himself had a short life on earth. Those who loved Him saw His agony from a brutal crucifixion and death to be a gut-wrenching tragedy. God saw it differently. He transformed this horrific event into the most thrilling miracle to ever happen in the universe. Death was defeated and the grave was no longer the permanent destination for God's people.

Our Living God is the giver of eternal life and no miracle on earth can be the equivalent of that. Yet, He places His healing power on the lives of those whose stories must continue for His kingdom's purpose. I live in celebration that that has happened for Jennifer, and my faith tells me that God is weaving His master plan in the lives of others, even when death comes to them early.

Search God's Word and you will read the testimonies of imperfect people who have had victorious lives because they belonged to Him. They experienced failures, tragedies, triumphs, and also miracles. God turned their ashes into beauty as He walked with them the entire time.

You also have a testimony to share with the world. Look at your own life and see where you may have experienced God's protection so your story could continue. Share this with your family, friends, and even with the hungry hearts of strangers who God places in your path.

It is in the midst of your hardships that room has been made for miracles. Let the knowledge of them be recognized and celebrated, as God's kingdom is called forth and His angels stand next to you.

*Jenny and Wynonna, "singing with their earth angels"

*This picture was taken 6/2023 when Jennifer met Wynonna at her concert.

Barbara J. Cornelius

<u>Psalm 20:5</u>

May we shout for joy over your victory and lift up our banners in the name of our God. May the LORD grant all your requests.

<u>Deuteronomy 31:8</u>

The LORD himself goes before you and will be with you; he will never leave you nor forsake you. Do not be afraid; do not be discouraged.

<u>Genesis 9:12-13</u>

And God said, "I am giving you a sign as evidence of my eternal covenant with you and all living creatures. I have placed my rainbow in the clouds. It is the sign of my permanent promise to you and to all of the earth."

Chapter Four

The Rainbow House

One dream had ended and another was just beginning. Chris and Hannah had been married nine years when their dream of becoming parents was finally coming true. However, after their experiencing twelve weeks of exuberance, Hannah had a miscarriage. This loss brought enormous emotional pain, but they had profound faith in the promise that their child would wait for them in heaven.

The decision was made that a short vacation in a rented a cabin might be the right environment for their spirits to begin healing. One morning as Chris and Hannah sat on the porch of the cabin, they began to talk about their future dream home. The welcoming porch reminded them that it was their number one requirement for a new home.

The house they had owned the past two years was comfortable, but it did not have a front porch and some of the other features they wanted. It was, after all, their starter home, but they were grateful to have it.

After returning from their short vacation, they happily continued to speculate about the features of their dream home. Chris decided to do a goggle search for houses in their area matching their requirements. Why not? It was just for fun. After looking at several pictures, they found one that made their eyes light up. Although the home was only around twelve years old, it had the look of a much older home. It also had a large front porch that was so typical of houses built almost a century ago. One other feature spoke to their hearts in a special way. The house was painted yellow. The nursery they had planned for their baby was going to be decorated in colors of yellow and grey.

The information on the house was limited. Chris and Hannah could not tell if it was currently on the market, and they had no idea what the price would be if it was. However, their close friend Robert was a realtor, so they decided to use his expertise in this impromptu search.

Robert discovered the home was in foreclosure and needed some "tender-loving care." After further investigation he determined the house to be structurally sound, needing only some cosmetic restoration. Most important, he thought buying it would be a prudent investment. To underscore how good a deal this might be, he said, "If you don't buy the house, I'm going to purchase it myself." Chris and Hannah, greatly encouraged by their friend's confidence, felt they would be up to the challenge of restoring the yellow house.

When Chris and Hannah went for their first look, they were greeted with the spectacular sight of a double rainbow over the house. Having asked God to guide their search, they wondered if this was a sign of His approval. Was He encouraging them? Looking at replacing the flooring, painting several rooms, and everything else which needed renovation, none of it translated into discouragement. Instead, what they saw was God's favor and a opportunity to be in a house of His choosing. Chris and Hannah's excitement over the house began to diminish their grief.

Chris had the carpentry skills to master the drawbacks of the neglected house, and with their realtor friend recommending a price that was in their budget, they prayerfully proceeded. Their friend knew Chris and Hannah needed to see other houses before making the final decision. Since it was the 4th of July week-end, it was agreed that they would all go to view houses two days later.

After enjoying time with his family, Robert took them to three different houses ranging in price from below the bid price to several thousand above. How would this foreclosed home look in comparison?

Upon going back to the yellow house, they were greeted by another double rainbow! Had Chris and Hannah not encouraged their friend to put family first and them second, they might not have seen this encouraging visual planted by God. His timing is perfect, and He gifted their trust with this confirmation.

Chris and Hannah decided to go forward with an offer for the "rainbow house." The bank declined their amount but informed them there would be one more opportunity to make a bid, and two other couples were also competing. They wondered if Daniel in the Old Testament, who had only one chance to interpret a dream, could be an inspiration for prayerfully determining the winning amount. King Nebuchadnezzar had given his wise men one chance to not only interpret his dream, but to also describe it. The penalty for failure was death. This sounded like an impossible request. The wise men thought they were doomed.

Daniel then asked God to tell him what the king had dreamed and what meaning was attached to it. When God answered his prayer, the lives of Daniel and the wise men were saved. The beautiful words of gratitude by Daniel gave all glory to God for this revelation. Of course, in Chris and Hannah's circumstance what was at stake was just purchasing a home and failure would be the loss of a dream- not precious lives. Would God reveal to them what they did not know and help them decide on the amount they needed to put forth? Of more eternal significance, would God give them a testimony about His participation in the daily concerns of His people today? Yes! Yes!

The amount offered by them was accepted, but that was just the beginning of the story God was writing for them. Chris and Hannah had prudently taken the steps for loan preapproval, but by the time their bid was accepted, their finances on paper looked differently to the bank. Some of their income was now coming not just from salaried income, but also from commissions. Now that they had signed a contract for their home, there was no longer approval of a loan by the bank. End of story? No, just God making a way through rough terrain to grow their faith even more.

When they spoke to the bank employee assigned to their loan application, she told them, "I can't approve your loan, but I can definitely see you living there." She suggested that they hire a mortgage broker to help them get the financing they needed. Her encouraging words were just what they needed to hear in the midst of learning their loan application had been declined. Yes, God's favor was still there, guiding their way.

When Chris and Hannah met with this financial expert, he told them, "Bear with me. This is a long arduous process, but if you stay the course, we can do this." It sounded like he had spoken from experience, and he had also repeated the words Apostle Paul shared with discouraged Christians many times. "Stay the Course." Feeling that they had again received affirmation from the Lord that He was guiding their way, they continued to prayerfully move forward.

It was helpful that their broker had prepared them for what they would go through. Sixty days of daily contact with him, submitting forms, collaborating documents, and tests of endurance for all involved was the path they travelled. They bathed all of this with a powerful weapon- prayer. Every single day for two months, Chris and Hannah walked in a circle around the yellow house and planted their prayers.

Another very important part of their dream coming to fruition was selling their current home. They were risking being homeless if they sold it and then could not buy the new one. A couple had indeed signed a contract on their current home. When Chris and Hannah finally received approval for their loan, a closing date was set.

This sounds like a perfect ending to the story. However, God was not through writing this thrilling testimony which would bless many others when Chris and Hannah shared it through the years. The day of the closing, the couple buying their home did not show up. The buyers had decided that there were three more minor changes that needed to happen before they would sign the papers. The bank gave Chris and Hannah an extension of only twenty-four hours. If they did not sign off then, they would lose the house.

Thankfully, all three requests were completed as they continued to pack up their belongings. It was agreed that the couple buying their home would electronically sign the closing papers by the end of the deadline. As the hours ticked by, Hannah and Chris who now had only a few hours left to realize their dream, finished loading their U-Haul truck and headed to their new home. Chris drove the truck and Hannah followed in their car.

As Chris drove toward the house, something strange happened. He noticed that even though it was a very hot summer day, the temperature in the unairconditioned cab became very cold. If that was not enough to heighten his anxiety, while traveling down a steep hill, he was met by a large, oncoming truck moving toward his lane. After it blew by without hitting him, the temperature in his truck normalized. Chris had felt a heaviness hanging over him the past few weeks, but now it was gone. Relief! Joyful peace! God had just given him a gift that he will never forget. He had allowed him to have a vivid, sensual experience that represented the spiritual battle he and Hannah were in as they sought to claim their house.

After Chris arrived ahead of Hannah, he saw that they had one hour left. Would they move into their dream home, or would they end up with just a truck full of all their possessions and no home? Feeling the power of the Holy Spirit, Chris sat on the porch, and prayed, "Lord, please give us entry into our home." Moments later, his cell phone rang and he learned that all signatures were in place and everything had been finalized. Victory in the Lord! God had made all the unpredictable, stress-filled, rough places smooth. When this part of their journey was finished, it became clear that God had gone ahead of them to prepare the way. God had turned their ashes into something beautiful — testimony of how He had acted on their behalf.

Chris and Hannah have now lived in their yellow dream house for one year. There have been no more double rainbows during that time, but there has been one single rainbow. Perhaps, the significance of the single rainbow was God giving them a sign that His spectacular promise of a child would be fulfilled. This young couple, after ten years of marriage, are now expecting another baby.

Their spacious home currently has three finished bedrooms on the first level, and a large unfinished area upstairs. It is more space than they need today, but not more than what they will need in the future where God has stored more blessings for them.

Chris and Hannah have been lovingly making physical changes to enhance their home. More important, every part of the house has been drenched in prayer and is filled with the promise and assurance of God's favor. The future holds the laughter of the new expected baby and that of other children who will be born and come to live in this house of rainbows. All generations of this family will celebrate and praise God for how He lovingly placed them in their "rainbow house." Their story will be a memory stone in their faith walk with the living God for the rest of their lives. Yay God!

God gives us encouraging signs that He is watching over us. These are His postmarks, just like the ones the postal service uses to indicate that our packages and letters are under their care. Rainbows are the most prominent of God's postmarks, but He continuously sends others to encourage us.

We can recognize them when difficult circumstances suddenly resolve, we receive words of encouragement during a stressful time in our lives, we receive unexpected favor from a person or business, something that been lost is miraculously found, and in numerous situations in our everyday lives. Look for them and observe how God is using them to make beauty out of your ashes. and praise Him for them!

Praise God! He is worthy! He is awesome! Tell the world!

35

<u>James 1:17</u>

Every good gift and every perfect gift is from above, coming down from the Father of lights with whom there is no variation of shadow due to change. Whatever is good and perfect is a gift coming down to us from God our Father, who created all the lights in the heavens.

Chapter Five

The Perfect Gift

When Larry and I married, we each had different ideas about gift giving. I wanted a present for every special occasion and especially for my birthday and Christmas. That expectation was quite burdensome for someone who was not used to that *ritual*. It did not seem to be a problem when we dated, but it definitely showed up when I was no longer his girlfriend, but his wife.

When we had been married eighteen months, Larry graduated from Purdue University and accepted a position as a small animal resident at Angell Memorial Hospital in Boston, Massachusetts. A few months after we moved, the time to commemorate my birthday arrived. It was the first time for me to celebrate without my family in Indiana, and I waited all day for Larry to come home. He finally arrived around 9:00 at night after a very long day at the hospital, and it immediately became clear to me that he had no idea what was special about that day. My response was to shed many tears and look for some reassurance from him that he would do something to make amends. He simply became angry that I thought it was such a big deal.

Somehow over the years the two of us switched places about our philosophy on exchanging presents. I began to realize Larry's failure to purchase gifts for me and my feelings being hurt over and over was not of any benefit to either of us. So, I began telling him what I desired for my birthday and

Christmas or, I bought it myself and then informed him of my purchase.

Eliminating the stress of his having to guess what gift would make me happy and then coming up empty handed, was a great relief to both of us. Certainly, this plan was a lot more satisfying to me, because I could then get what I really wanted. I tried to persuade Larry to do the same thing, so he could also have something he would enjoy. That occasionally resulted in nothing for him, but he didn't seem to mind. He was just happy to be "off the hook" from the old arrangement. It took me way, way too long to realize what the problem had been for him in all the disappointing years of exchanging gifts. Larry simply didn't know what I would like. He also wanted the gift to be a surprise *and* perfect. That sometimes resulted in *no* gift. Throughout the years he became much more aware of what would make me happy and very thoughtful about his choices. I on the other hand became very lackadaisical about it all as I realized he showed his love toward me in other, wonderful ways.

One day after we had been married for over forty years, I got a really big surprise! I had been out of town for several days when, on my first day back home, I received a call from a salesman at our local Toyota dealership. He asked me, "Do you want the top for your new convertible to be black or khaki?" (The salesman had not realized it was supposed to be a surprise.) I was absolutely stunned, because Larry had always been so cost-conscious and he also was very conservative in his choices. We had always driven station wagons, vans, or fuel-efficient smaller cars. I promptly tried to talk Larry out of this purchase, but I did not succeed. He said I had been talking for thirty years about getting a convertible when I retired from teaching. Since I had recently done just that, he wanted to bring my dream to fruition. Honestly, I was always joking about that desire. It was just fun to say it to others.

Boy was I happy I failed to change his mind! This red convertible (I chose a black top because we were in Georgia Bulldogs territory) gave me a new *persona*. I became the coolest sixty some years old lady in the neighborhood and even in other parts of Georgia. When I was much younger, I would laugh at all the old people I saw in convertibles. I loved it that the laugh was now on me!

When I put the top down and picked up a grandchild from middle school, they and their friends really appreciated me! I had waited decades to be *admired* in that way and it was a lot of fun. I even had people strike up conversations with me about my red convertible when I was at gas stations and parking lots.

When our two oldest grandchildren earned their driver's licenses, they each had the privilege of driving Meemaw's neat car. It became a rite of passage. The other six grandchildren arc now eagerly waiting for their turns. None of them seem to mind that this car is now fifteen years old, and has none of the modern technology. Evidently red convertibles never go out of style.

Even when long-time friends visited us, they also wanted to ride in my snazzy car and have their pictures taken to commemorate the occasion. Maybe they also had secret long-time dreams similar to mine. When I look at these photographs from years ago, they make me smile. I am not sure Larry anticipated all the years of enjoyment I would get from his purchase. He most certainly made up for the "missing" gifts from years ago!

Today Larry's surprise gift sits next to my practical car, a Toyota Highlander, in my garage in the retirement community where I now live alone. No one here seems to have a "cool" car like mine, and I am pretty confident that it is of no concern to any of them. Still, I really like having one in my old age, even if no one here cares a whit about that kind of stuff. Little did I know all those years ago, when I was young, that I would someday be a little old lady with a red convertible!

Although I drive it infrequently, I still get a lot of pleasure when I do. I have entertained the idea of selling it, but I just can't bring myself to do it. It was Larry's special gift to me, and I remember all the fun we had with it. It was a symbol of his love for me, and he was extremely pleased with himself when he gave it to me. There is something about putting others' desires and needs at the forefront of your life that makes you happy in return. Remembering Larry doing that for me is something I will always treasure. It is in those moments that I see how the ashes of my previous disappointments have turned into a beautiful memory, and that is exactly what the Lord wanted me to see.

Look at the memories you have of a loved one who is no longer with you, and praise God for the time you were given with them. God's Word promises that if they belonged to Him, it is not the end of your story with them. Larry and I will be together again in the presence of our Savior. All sadness will fade away, and the Lord will replace it with immeasurable joy. That is the truly perfect gift God gives to all of His children.

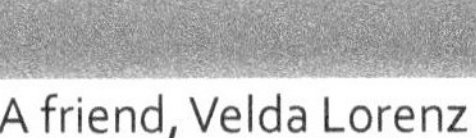

A friend, Velda Lorenz

Grandson Benjamin Snipes

Grandaughter
Alyssa Wyatt

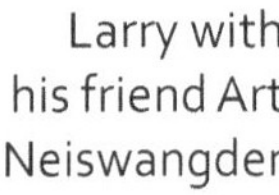

Larry with
his friend Art
Neiswangder

Colossians 2:2-3

I want you woven into a tapestry of love, in touch with everything there is to know of God. Then you will have minds confident and at rest, focused on Christ, God's great mystery.

Revelation 21:4

He will wipe away every tear from their eyes, and death shall be no more, neither shall there be mourning, nor crying, nor pain anymore, for the former things have passed away.

John 14:1-2

Let not your heart be troubled: ye believe in God, believe also in me. In my Father's house are many mansions if it were not so, I would have told you. I go to prepare a place for you.

Chapter Six

A Family Made from Memories Lost

The patients in a recently opened memory care unit were new to their surroundings and their plight was heart-breaking for their families. They were a shadow of their former selves, and they were slowly leaving their loved ones as their brains developed neurological roadblocks. Still, something memorable and heart-warming happened in the midst of this situation. Memories lost from cognition impairment can be replaced with new ones in unlikely places, when God makes beauty from ashes. This is a story of one of God's miracles in the presence of despair.

Fewer than ten patients resided in the recently opened memory care facility where families had tearfully placed each one. There were many challenging issues facing the medical staff: the impossible ideal of having a health care worker for each individual, the selection of effective resources for patients experiencing a slow decline in their physical and mental abilities, and the management of the ensuing emotional turmoil when no solution brings normalcy. It is then when the Holy Spirit can soothe aching spirits and give hope not based on what is seen, but that which is believed.

Families had put pictures of their loved ones and me-

mentos in shadow boxes outside their rooms. They were to remind anyone who walked by that a precious soul with a life that mattered resided there. These new residents had once been very accomplished in their lives. Sadly, their years of productivity seemed to be in the past, and melancholy had now become their constant companion. On occasion one of them would quietly say, "I want to go home." Home had been a place that brought feelings of being safe and secure. It could no longer be found here on earth, but was the place where their lost loved ones resided. It was there that God had prepared a heavenly manor for them, and where they would surpass any excellence achieved on earth. Restoration and renewal awaited them.

In the interim, there were many battles yet to be endured by the patients and their families. Daily, family members looked for opportunities to participate in the lives of their diminished dear ones. It was important the residents know how much they were still cherished. All the time left on this side of eternity, although it was filled with tremendous stress and difficulty, was measured and greatly treasured. None of these families wanted the good-byes that were coming. Saying goodbye to the suffering would be a relief, but not saying goodbye to the person who had become an irreplaceable part of their lives.

In the midst of all this heartache, God created comfort in a surprising and unique way in the aching spirits of the families and patients. Something beautiful took up residence in this place of sadness. None of them were alone. The Holy Spirit which resided in the hearts of these patients, families and medical staff was also present.

There were occasions when families could see glimpses of their loved one's former selves. The humanity of all of them was still present and was making itself known. One particular patient would occasionally sit at the piano and play by memory some of the music she had once shared with many others in her church. Another patient who had a medical background cautioned a very feeble man about trying to stand up from his wheelchair by calling out, "No. You need to sit back down so you don't fall." Never mind that this former doctor was also in a wheelchair. He was still a person who takes care of others. Yet another patient using a walker could see a friend struggling and saying he wanted to leave. This kind man who had been known to always help others in need, said "I will take you where you want to go." Of course, there was no way for that to happen.

As people congregated in the large room provided for visitation, a spirit of oneness began to evolve. A "We are Family" plaque was lovingly placed by the wife of one of the patients on the credenza under the television. Other relatives took pictures of this "new family" and posted them on a bulletin board in the room. One of the patients frequently looked for her picture when she entered the room. Perhaps seeing it was a message to her that she still mattered in this world.

Sometimes a staff member would patiently sit and play a simple card game with some of the patients. Occasionally when the activities director brought balls to toss to the seated patients, family members felt comfortable enough to join them. Many of the patients and their visitors frequently watched sports events, movies, and sitcoms together. Being able to continue sharing their lives with each other was a gift received in gratitude by all of them.

Playful interaction became natural for the residents and family members. One male patient who had not laughed in a long time, reared his head back in laughter as he reacted to comments made by one of the female patients. She had always been very witty and a great sense of humor was still a part of her personality. Frequently her comment about a confusing circumstance was, "Oh dear." This brought smiles to everyone present. Sometimes, creating happiness can be a "team sport" and deliciously contagious, and that was evident in this situation. Life had been reduced to simple pleasures that no one wanted to miss. Savoring was the focus now.

This lightheartedness flowed over to the dining area where animated conversations at meal time became the norm. The familiarity bred not only elation, but also created natural affection among all of the people present. Occasionally a prayer by a family member was offered to bless a meal, and that somehow made it feel more like home. The tapestry of heart-breaking circumstances brought everyone together.

One fall evening after dinner two young nursing assistants decided that the dirty dishes on the tables could wait awhile. The assistants took some of the patients, followed by their family members, out to the courtyard to enjoy the fresh air and the setting sun. These two young women prioritized what mattered in those precious moments. One spouse commented sometime later, "One of my last memories of my husband was sitting beside him in the courtyard that evening and witnessing the peaceful expression on his face. I felt like I was getting a preview of what it will be like when the two of us are together in heaven. This memory now gives me great comfort."

Some of the patients are now on the other side of eternity. God tells us in Revelation 21:5 that He makes all things new. This means when we go home to Him, we are completely restored! All the physical limitations that hindered these patients from being themselves are now completely gone. Their gifts, abilities, and personalities which made them who they were have been restored. Nothing has been lost, but is now instead magnified in their heavenly spirits. As they dwell in their new home in the presence of the Living God, they wait for their family members still on earth to join them. The end for them does not exist. Everything is just beginning.

Although heavy grief is a constant companion for those left behind, they know they are not alone. Their Heavenly Father is holding them and their weary spirits in His arms. Witnessing how He acted on the behalf of their loved ones during their last days gives them hope for what is in their own future. They believe they have not lost forever those who are no longer in their sight. They know exactly where they are and that a victorious reunion is waiting for all of them. God will change all their ashes of mourning into a beauty that cannot be seen on earth. It will be worth the waiting.

We are family.

<u>Isaiah 43:4</u>

Since you are precious and honored in my sight, and because I love you, I will give people in exchange for you, nations in exchange for your life.

<u>Psalm 139:14-15</u>

I will praise you, for I am fearfully and wonderfully made; your works are wonderful, I know that full well. My frame was not hidden from You, when I was made in the secret place, when I was woven together in the depths of the earth.

<u>Ephesians 1:4</u>

Even before he made the world, God loved us and chose us in Christ to be holy and without fault in his eyes.

Chapter Seven
Your Life Is Like a Delicious Pie

"You are a remarkable woman," were the words spoken to me after the service for my mother-in-law. I had successfully given her eulogy and honored this woman whom I had called Mother for over forty years. My response to this extravagant compliment was, "You saw one slice of my pie. You saw the right slice." This person hadn't seen me when, an hour before the service, I sat in an office at the funeral home and sobbed. With my sorrow so deeply felt, I had enormous doubt that I would be able to deliver my prepared speech. However, releasing my tears in those moments enabled me to have a clear mind and the strength to speak for the family about a very exceptional woman.

I believe everyone's life is like a pie in that some slices make it to the serving dish in one nice-looking piece while others, fall apart as they are placed there. The pie is not ruined because some of it is not visually appealing. It is still delicious. Just like a pie, we all have some marvelous pieces (attributes) along with some that are not so superb. The ones that are not commendable do not erase our worth in this universe. They do not represent the whole of us. God looks at our entire being and allows the mistakes we make to become part of a beautiful tapestry of our lives. He makes beauty from our "ashes."

I have always been greatly encouraged that God's Word reveals a truthful and complete picture of those He chose to be His mighty leaders. King David is one of my favorites. He was a young teenager when he defiantly stepped before Goliath to end his taunting of Israel. He had practiced his courage many times when he protected his sheep from wild animals, so he was able to be fearless when he "stood toe to toe" before the giant. His heroic words, spoken with the confidence of great faith, are recorded in 1 Samuel:17, "You come to me with a sword and with a spear and with a javelin, but I come to you in the name of the Lord of hosts, the God of the armies of Israel, whom you have defied." With one smooth stone in his slingshot, he brought down the mighty giant. David was described in the Old Testament as a man after God's own heart. Yet, he was estranged from God at one point in his life when he turned into a murderer.

David had committed adultery with Bathsheba who was Uriah the Hittite's wife. She had become pregnant and David was desperate to find a way to escape his predicament. He decided the solution to his problem was to have Uriah killed. David later acknowledged his loathsome, ungodly behavior and throughout his life he endured tragedies that evolved from his actions. His story did not end with his destructive behavior. He received restoration when he repented of his reprehensible behavior, thus restoring his relationship with God.

Many of the heartfelt psalms written by David came from his despair over what he had done and the consequences he experienced the rest of his life. Yet, God's Word tells of the victories David had with the Lord throughout his remaining days. Scripture reveals his worthiness through God's eyes, and His heart for David was not blotted out by the darkness of the sin. David wrote over half of the Psalms in the Bible. Many times, when I read them, I say to myself, "How could David so accurately describe the emotional pain I am feeling today?" I am greatly comforted by his words three thousand years after he wrote them.

Another person in the Old Testament who had a very close relationship with God was Moses. God chose Moses to lead nearly two million Hebrews out of their bondage in Egypt to the promised land. Scripture says that the LORD even spoke to him face to face. Moses was so important to

God's plan of salvation for His people that he, along with the prophet Elijah, appeared at the transfiguration of Jesus on Mount Tabor. Matthew 17:2 describes Jesus's face as shining like the sun and his clothes becoming as white as the light. Incredulously, Jesus, Moses, and Elijah were together on that mountain. Moses and the prophet Elijah had left this earth a few thousand years earlier, but there they were having a conversation with Jesus about what was to come.

Looking back to when Moses was a young man in Egypt, we see a different kind of man. Exodus 2:11-12 says "One day after Moses had grown up, he went out to where his own people were and watched them at their hard labor. He saw an Egyptian beating a Hebrew, one of his own people. Glancing this way and that and seeing no one, he killed the Egyptian and hid him in the sand." This murder did not define the entire story of Moses and sentence him to a life of degradation and shame. It caused him to retreat to the desert for forty years where God "grew him up" to be His person. He then was able to courageously challenge Pharaoh and rescue the Hebrew people from slavery in Egypt.

God can use anyone for His purpose and shock the world. He did this with a woman who became an unlikely heroine in the Old Testament. The story of the prostitute Rahab should encourage anyone who feels that their past destroys any chance of their having a victorious future. When Joshua sent two spies to scout out Jericho, Rahab hid them as they are about to be discovered. She shared with them why she was willing to take a risk that could cost her own life. She said," The idols of Jericho are worthless, but the God who parted the Red Sea for Israel when they fled the bondage of Egypt, is the powerful Living God of the universe." Rahab recognized the two men as His messengers. When the walls of Jericho supernaturally fell after the Israelites marched around the city for seven days, Rahab was saved to finish her story.

She married Salmon and their child was Boaz. Boaz married Ruth and their child was Obed who became the father of Jesse. Jesse became the father of King David. This lineage continued unto the birth of Jesus. Would anyone living in the time of Rahab, knowing she was a prostitute, have had any idea of her worth to our Lord? No way. It doesn't matter what the world thought about her. It only mattered what God saw in her.

Then in the New Testament in Acts 9:1-6 is the story

of Saul who became Paul. Saul ravaged the church, entered house after house, and dragged men and women from their homes and put them in prison. He was deeply dedicated to persecuting all Christians until he met Jesus on his way to Damascus. There in the midst of his journey, Jesus spoke to him in a blinding light shining from heaven. "Saul, Saul, why are you persecuting Me?" When Saul asked, "Who are You Lord?" Jesus identified Himself and said, "I am Jesus, Whom you are persecuting."

Miraculously, after this encounter, Saul was transformed into a new man named Paul, an apostle for Christ. Paul could have retreated into a life of shame for his heinous deeds before he met the Lord. Instead, he repented and was redeemed by the Lord. He spent the rest of his life, embodied with God's Spirit, delivering the message of salvation to the world. For over thirty years, he endured tremendous hardship and physical torment to spread the Good News. He was passionate about Jesus right up to the day he was executed.

Paul's story is told in the several books he wrote in the New Testament and his testimony after two thousand years is still bringing people to the Lord. Those who observed Saul when he was terrorizing Christians could not have possibly seen who he was to become. God had a plan for his life that the world could not have thought possible. The world does not have God's eyes. Paul's dark days as Saul did not define him; they gave contrast to who he became in Christ.

What does your "pie" look like? Can you examine your previous mistakes, current shortcomings, and sins too heavy to bear and still realize who you are in Christ? They do not define your life in Him. Christ paid for all of your imperfections when He died on the cross. There is not one sin that he did not pay for when He suffered the great agony of crucifixion and gave up His life for you. If we confess those sins, we experience forgiveness and a new life in our Lord. We become a redeemed child of God.

Your story is unique and is not defined by your past. It is highlighted by God's call on your life, and only you can tell it. You were meant to touch the lives of others in ways that will remain mostly unknown to you until you go home to be with the Lord. Be certain, you are meant to live in victory as the Lord turns your ashes into something beautiful that will last for eternity!

Romans 8:28

All things work together for good to them that love God, to them who are the called according to his purposes.

Luke 16:10a

If you are faithful in little things, you will be faithful in large things.

Chapter Eight
Santa Claus Invades Seniors'
Christmas Party

The fellowship hall in our church had never looked more uninviting, disorganized, and just plain dirty. The floor was covered with debris from numerous craft activities, the tables were coated with syrup from a pancake breakfast, and several boxes of miscellaneous materials for numerous hands-on activities sat on the floor. Yet in this place, an adult Christmas Party was scheduled to begin in just over an hour!

The breakfast with Santa which had just taken place was a rousing success for the children, thanks to the adults who had participated with much love and devotion. The condition of the room was proof that the event had had an explosion of happiness! The huge mess meant that many sets of children's hands had experienced fun with the creative materials provided! This special event had even been commemorated by pictures taken with Santa. These pictures would be kept as "memory stones" for families to treasure for many years.

Most important of all, our church had invited the children of the community to celebrate Jesus in the midst of the Christmas season. A message about the love Jesus brought to earth was embedded in everything that took place. However, there was no time to savor the success and *slowly* remove the remnants of a fantastic morning! Senior citizens lead by me were breathing down Santa's neck.

We had not been participants in this spirit-filled project, and felt some desperation about the housekeeping that needed to be accomplished in ninety minutes. Our Sunday School Class's Christmas party was supposed to begin in that short period of time, and we had a lot of work to do: empty the large room of all trash, remove boxes, vacuum, clean and decorate tables, put centerpieces and decorations in place, and prepare for the caterer who was arriving in thirty minutes. Normally most of this would have been done the day before, but because of the visitation with Santa, this was not possible.

How did this obviously, short-sighted planning fiasco happen? My committee had been diligent in placing our date on the church calendar a few months prior to our party. We had locked in a wonderful caterer, and jumped all the hurdles that come naturally when "middle school students" inhabit senior citizen bodies. (Trying to get a group of us to agree on date, time, location, and menu is a challenging task all by itself.) Then, a few weeks before our party, I received a call from the church office and was told there was a conflict with the date we had chosen. Someone had forgotten to put the Santa event on the calendar, and it was always done the first Saturday in December. Additionally, the wonderful man who was always Santa could not do it later, because he was scheduled for surgery the following week.

When I heard this latest development, my mind resonated with the words I had shared with the Sunday School Class when we began planning the party. I had piously reminded all of us that this was a celebration of our Lord's birth and we would make that our priority. Nothing was to take away from our celebrating the true meaning of Christmas and honoring our Lord.

Never did I think when I made that announcement that God with His great sense of humor, would test my mettle. I had already batted down the discontent of a few people with the decisions that had been made. As I said, we are pretty diverse in what we think encompasses a perfect party and also about any other subject that comes up.

Selecting another date and location was problematic during the Christmas season, and rescheduling the caterer was also a big problem. In addition to those concerns, some of us were no longer secure in driving at night and preferred lunch time for parties. Normally we would have just decided on a later time in the day, but we had promised all of us (yes that includes me) who were rabid football fans that everyone would be home that day in time to see the SEC Championship Football Game. Picky! Picky! Picky!

I don't know how many times I see Christians lose sight about the true meaning of Christmas over the smallest matters, and here I was about to do the very same thing. I didn't see this one coming. Our bubbly, optimistic (*think Pollyanna*) pastor led the way in finding a solution for the fellowship hall being accidentally double booked. She said she would make sure we had the assistance needed to transform the room quickly into a clean, neat, desirable space for our Christmas Party. (This lady has the faith of a spiritual giant and the track record with the Lord to back it up.)

My response to her (which was not my original response when I learned about the situation) was, "I can't wait to see what God is going to do with this "mashup" of a children's Santa Party and a senior citizen Christmas Party. God does like to give us challenges so we can appreciate His surprising, unpredictable outcomes.

Sure enough, many people from our class, from the "Breakfast with Santa" crew, and our sweet pastor worked together in a synchronized, harmonious rhythm to totally transform the room after Santa was finished. It was even done with a few minutes to spare. Had we set up the room the day before with a few adults, it definitely would have taken much longer. Motivation, cooperation, and desperation make all the difference in a challenging situation. Both events were beautifully done and enjoyed that day. Who knew that could happen under the stressful circumstances! God did.

I often reflect on the lovely memories of that day, and I realize God was teaching me a more important lesson than one of teamwork saving the day. Both events were held in a place that had been anointed by thousands of prayers: during church luncheons, wedding receptions, meals for families after funerals, Bible studies, and activities that involved every age group in our church. God always blesses the ground He has claimed. He certainly demonstrated this with all of us who participated in the two parties. God definitely turned my ashes into a beautiful experience that day.

Look in the Old Testament and you will see many thrilling examples of God claiming His territory in the world.

When God parted the Red Sea so the "trapped" Israelites could cross and escape the Egyptians breathing down their necks, when the walls of Jericho came tumbling down after seven days of Joshua leading God's people in a march around them, when Daniel escaped being killed in the lion's den, when Shadrach, Meshach, and Abednego survived a fiery furnace without even the smell of fire on their clothing, and when David killed Goliath, God revealed His mighty power in ways that the world could not grasp.

Before Moses led God's people across the newly created path in the Red Sea, before Joshua marched in faith with his people, before Daniel faced the menacing lions, before Shadrach, Meshack, and Abednego were tossed into a furnace, and before David killed Goliath, they had all practiced their faith in their daily lives. They knew about the character and power of God and realized that their belief in Him was rooted in *not* seeing their trials through the lens of the world, but through that of God's eyes. In all of these situations they had practiced walking the ground claimed by God.

Seek the ground that God has claimed by looking for it in everything you do. Events in your life that you see as unimportant are seen by God with a different perspective. He wants to be a part of all that you do. When this happens, He has access to your heart and spirit, and He can use you in a mighty way in His kingdom.

Practicing your faith in the daily small, seemingly insignificant events, prepares you to face formidable situations with courage. Where do you need to practice your courage today? Can you see your faith growing as you partner with God? Let God claim His ground in your life.

Bobbie & Jackie Duncan

Larry & I

Santa, Larry, & I

Wanda & David Hill

Lamar & Gayle Duncan

61

Matthew 18: 19-20

"Again, I say to you if two of you agree on earth concerning anything that they ask, it will be done for them by My Father in heaven. For where two or three are gathered together in My name, I am in the midst of them."

Philippians 4:6-7

Don't worry about anything: instead, pray about everything. Tell God what you need, and thank him for all he has done. Then you will experience God's peace, which exceeds anything we can understand. His peace will guard your hearts and minds as you live in Christ Jesus.

Chapter Nine

The Faltering Prayers of Human "Angels"

The heartfelt words of her prayer were spoken very slowly and tentatively. "Lord please heal Vera and make her well." It was one of the most beautiful prayers I had ever heard. It was softly delivered to our Heavenly Father by my mother. At the time of the prayer, she was over eighty years old. I realized I had no memory of her praying aloud like that before. More than twenty-five years have passed since my mother spoke that prayer. She is no longer living, but I can still hear her voice so very clearly as I think back to that time. It meant that much to me.

On that day there had been several of us family members standing in a circle around my mother-in-law who sat in a rocking chair. She had been suffering several debilitating health problems, and we wanted her to hear our personal prayers on her behalf. My mother was a very caring person with a tender heart, and had been a very dedicated nurse in obstetrics. For forty years she had lovingly assisted thousands of women bring their babies into this world. She had also had several heartbreaks over the years including the loss of my nine-year-old brother after a long illness, and thirty years later, the loss of her husband, my father, after he had had many years of poor health. Even though she had experienced much grief in her life, she still courageously lived her life with a strong faith.

I believe my mother was a "human" angel on this earth. She did not have wings, but her spoken words did. I had stood in church with her for all the years that I was growing up and received the blessing of saying the Lord's Prayer and other prayers with her during worship. I myself had only begun to speak audible, personal prayers for others when I was in my fifties.

My praying aloud began when I was in a Bible study at the church discussing an urgent need of our group leader who was not with us that evening. I said, "Someone needs to pray about this, right now!" No one offered to do this, and so I nervously said I would do it. I simply said aloud the thoughts I had had about what I wanted the Lord to do on behalf of our leader. I spoke very hesitantly because this experience was new to me. My heart was totally exposed to God. I believe that is exactly what He wanted.

I didn't possess the powerful words of a Billy Graham or some other well-known preacher. I didn't have flowery prayer language. I just needed to humbly speak about what was happening to someone our group loved so much. Stepping forward that day freed me to do this anytime when I was with others and there was a prayer request. I felt comfortable praying about any need. I had met a Christian friend many years ago who said, "Pray about everything. If you only wait for the big stuff, you won't have many conversations with God." Realizing that relationships grow with frequent, quality time, I began a life-long journey of getting to know my Lord.

My wonderful friend George at church taught me that when people ask for prayer, many times it needs to happen immediately and not go on a long prayer list. (Do most people really recall when someone has asked to be remembered in prayer?) He not only prayed his heart out in audible words, he also did it wherever he was. If you voiced a need to him, he would immediately stop and talk to the Lord on your behalf. On one occasion, I met George in the crowded hallway of a hospital where my husband was a patient. He inquired about how Larry was doing and I told him I was very worried. He then laid his hand on my arm and asked God to intercede on Larry's behalf. George created a space right there in that hallway for us to talk to our Lord, and I will never forget feeling the power of God in that moment. Our Lord was right there with us, and I know that because of that conversation with

God, Larry and I experienced many more years to be together. Thank you, Father.

When we look at Scripture in the Bible, we see many, many times that God's people prayed in an audible voice to Him in large public settings. Moses, God's prophets, the disciples, and the Apostle Paul did so. They created a space wherever they were to have a conversation with God and request Him to intercede in the urgent situation they were facing. Certainly, our Lord himself spoke to His Father in large groups. Sometimes, there were thousands present. In their midst He spoke to His Father in the most personal, loving way, showing us how to do the same thing.

Over seventeen years ago my family had the blessing of praying with many people in a public setting. My daughter Jennifer was in intensive care after having her baby delivered six weeks early in an attempt to save her life. We requested prayer from friends, family and anyone we could reach. The result was that almost thirty people stood in a circle in an open area near the intensive care area in the hospital and prayed aloud. Many beautiful, humble voices spoke words of faith and asked the Lord for the healing of my daughter and a testimony that would glorify Him. These wonderful people were like human angels to me. I feel certain that invisible, heavenly angels were also there.

Prior to the prayers of the large group at the hospital, I had had my private, personal time with the Lord. 2 Samuel 7:18 speaks of how King David went and sat in prayer before the LORD. He had so intimate of a relationship with God that He sought out those moments. I have always loved that Scripture, because it encourages me to also seek those very special times with God. Several times in the first critical hours of Jennifer's hospitalization, I had stood next to my daughter's bed and tearfully, fervently, prayed. I was prepared to accept His will as I begged for a miracle. I am so grateful for all of the private and public prayers offered on behalf of Jennifer. The words of these human "angels" took flight and the story of Jennifer's healing has been shared with hundreds of people these last seventeen years.

In the last years of our marriage my husband and I would wrap our arms around each other and pray aloud wherever we were. In his last days when his health was failing, he would frequently ask me to sit beside him and pray for him. Those moments are some of my most treasured ones. The value they have for me cannot be measured. God's beauty from ashes came in those times.

Prayers offered in your quiet moments with God are conversations that He wants. He asks us to create a space in the world to be with Him, whether it is in an intimate setting by ourselves or with a group who needs to shut out the world's distractions and be with Him. In those moments, we are in a supernatural "bubble" with Him. Our words whether they are quiet, hesitant, or even incoherent are gold to Him.

God valued us so much and desired a relationship with us so much that He sent His Son to rescue us. Be open to all the opportunities you have when the Holy Spirit prompts you to pray in private or in a public setting. Pray about everything. God wants to hear our words of praise, thanksgiving and those that tell Him the desires of our hearts. Watch Him turn your "ashes" into something of beauty that the world cannot comprehend.

Prayers to our Lord can sometimes happen in a "supernatural bubble." Find your special place to be alone with Him or in a group setting.

Make space for Him wherever you are.

A family prayer of thanksgiving

grandkids Alyssa and Brandon Wyatt
in bubbles

Prayer for My Lost Loved One

Christian Tagaloh/unsplash

Heavenly Father,

I place my loved one(s) under my umbrella of faith as I ask these things:

Bring in to captivity all his/her thoughts to your will. **(2 Corinthians 10:5)**

Give him/her a circumcised heart that he/she might know you. **(Deuteronomy 30:6)**

Soften his/her heart, that the spark of eternity You placed in his/her heart becomes a raging fire of faith in You. **(Ecclesiastes 3:11)**

Father, according to your word I prepare for battle on their behalf:

I take the shield of faith and with it extinguish every flaming dart of the evil one that would come against me, my family, and the one for whom I offer this prayer. **(Ephesians 6:16)**

I take the sword of the spirit, which is Your Word in prayer and with it I come against every power and principality that would set itself against me, my family and the one for whom I pray. **(Ephesians 6:17)**

As a prayer warrior for You, I call forth Your kingdom throughout my home, my family, and my domain. I pray this in the name of Jesus Christ, with all glory and honor and thanks to You.

Amen

Barbara J. Cornelius

Putting On the Armor of God

Good morning, Father! Good morning, Jesus! Good morning, Holy Spirit!

<u>**Romans 12:1**</u>

Heavenly Father, according to your word, I present my body as a living sacrifice, holy, acceptable in thy sight.

<u>**Ephesians 6: 14-17**</u>

Now, Father, I gird my loins about with truth to protect me from all lies and errors told to me, about me or by me to myself.

I put on the breastplate of righteousness to protect myself from all sinful and evil desires.

I shod my feet with the preparation of the gospel of peace and ask that you would give me a hunger for your word and a zeal for your word, that I might live your word and spread your word and your peace.

Above all, I take the shield of faith and with it I extinguish every flaming dart of the evil one that would come against me or my family.

I take the helmet of salvation to protect my mind and my body from accident, calamity and infirmity.

I take the sword of the spirit, which is the word of God in prayer and with it I come against every power and principality that would set itself against me, my family, or my church.

<u>Isaiah 58:8</u>

And, according to your Word, the glory of the Lord is my rear guard.

Now Heavenly Father, I praise you and thank you for the armor that you have provided for me to dress in this day. I am completely covered in the name of Jesus, according to your word, Father.

Morning Prayer

Matthew 16:18

Upon Jesus I have built my life, my home, and my marriage, and the gates of hell shall not prevail against it.

Psalm 23:1	You are my shepherd, I shall not want.
Philippians 4:13	I can do all things through Christ who strengthens me.
2 Corinthians 10:5	I cast down all imaginations, and bring into captivity every evil thought,
1 Peter 5:7	and I cast all my care upon you, for you careth for me.
Psalm 103:3	I praise you for walking in divine health, for you are my God and you healeth all my diseases,
Isaiah 53:5	and by your stripes I am healed.
3 John 2	I just praise you and thank you for my prosperity and good health, even as my soul prospers.
Nehemiah 8:10	For the joy of the Lord is my strength.

<u>**Jeremiah 1:12**</u>   Father, I have prayed according to your Word, and
You have said you would watch over your Word to perform it.

Father, just rise up and live big within me today, for I am yours, in the name of Jesus.   Amen.

Barbara J. Cornelius

<u>Isaiah 40:3-4</u>

The voice of one crying in the wilderness: "Prepare the way of the Lord; make straight in the desert a highway for our God. Every valley shall be exalted and every mountain and hill brought low, the crooked places shall be made straight and the rough places smooth."

Chapter Ten
I Rode a Bus with Jesus

When seeking entertainment, long bus trips are the least desired mode of transportation for us senior citizens. In addition to the distaste for spending many hours on a bus, there's the reality that some of us are "middle school students" in old bodies. We share similar, challenging attributes with those youngsters: short attention spans, impatience, and wild variance in attitudes and emotional states. (I joyously taught middle schoolers for over thirty years, and I was equally "yoked" with my students.)

Yet, my husband and I traveled in a bus with like-minded people for a ten-hour-trip to see the Creation Museum and Ark Encounter. I had told Larry that seeing these two things was at the top of my bucket list, and in a moment of weakness, he agreed to go. I anticipated having a rewarding spiritual experience when we visited the two Christian sites, but I suspect Larry was just hoping for survival. I say that because there was a lot of moaning and groaning coming from his direction before we left. Being inexperienced travelers, we were surprised at the unexpected obstacles that came our way. The prolonged hours in the cramped space on the bus certainly made fertile ground for us quickly recognizing negative possibilities!

The first day began with an optimistic prayer by the pastor of the church sponsoring the trip. He also happened to be the husband of our energetic and bubbly tour leader. The heart-felt requests in his prayer turned out to be more of a necessity than we had ever imagined, but they also provided wonderful opportunities to see God at work in surprising ways.

We began our first few hours on the bus with lots of snacks (it was like being on a small cruise ship resting on land instead of water). We also saw an inspirational movie about the famous horse Secretariat, and sang many songs to the accompaniment of the pastor's guitar. We pretty much sang in tune and were very creative in our remembrance of the lyrics.

Rambunctious as some in our group were, we still managed good behavior for the most part in the presence of not one, but two pastors. We came to know that the person who gave a devotional each day on the bus was a spirit-filled pastor, thirty years counting, of an African-American church. This man spoke with the authority of Moses. Now, I will have to wait until I get my "promotion in heaven" to know this, but I am pretty sure he was that good.

It turns out that we needed the prayerful guidance of "Moses" on the first day of our trip. We didn't need the Red Sea parted by God, but we did have an adventure with a bridge that had collapsed along our route. Thankfully, we were not on the bridge when it gave way, and it didn't result in any fatalities (unless you count the attitudes of our bus driver, the administrators who ran the bus company, our tour leader, and some of the other passengers upon receiving the news about the bridge).

Because of this obstacle we were projected to arrive at our hotel two hours later than the scheduled time and that created a problem involving the bus driver. To arrive at our destination for the night, he would exceed the maximum hours he was allowed to drive. After speaking with his supervisor, he informed our fearless (and I do mean fearless) leader that we would need to find new reservations for all forty-five of us to spend the night. Knowing that we had already prepaid for our designated hotel, our tour leader sitting next to her pastor/husband spoke up in her beautiful southern accent and said *that* was not happening. This assertion did not make for a harmonious relationship with our disgruntled driver, who, although he looked to be in his sixties, was not a kindred spirit with his "middle school passengers." Our leader evidently spoke with great authority, because after our driver talked to his boss a second time, we continued on our trip and arrived at our hotel late that evening.

The second day began with our bus driver giving a sincere apology for his grumpiness the previous day, and we began again with renewed hopes and aspirations for seeing God at work. God had after all, parted our sea of deep discontent. This allowed all of us to arrive at the next location in our journey without the bus driver quitting! Yay!

Compared to the first day, the second was pretty uneventful and devoid of irritating experiences. It was however, a spectacular day in terms of spiritual blessings. We stopped at a famous horse farm in Kentucky, and unfortunately one of the ladies got too close to a feisty horse and she suffered a bite on her arm. The puncture went through the sleeve of her jacket and made an impressive bruise. I was close by and I asked her if I could pray for her injured arm, and she readily accepted. Jesus always shows up when we invite him, and His spirit was felt right there in our midst. I feel certain that the complete healing of her arm which came later, became a testimony from her trip.

Seeing several white stallions at the farm made me think about Scripture in the Book of Revelation which says Jesus will return to earth on a white horse. One stallion in particular was much larger than the others. Maybe the stunning animal upon which our triumph Savior will sit will look like this majestic white horse. I definitely had a huge God moment in reflecting about that possibility. After touring this farm and seeing several horses being exercised by their jockeys on the race track, we then made our way to the Creation Museum.

Arriving at this location caused all of us to remember why we had gotten on the bus in the first place. The museum's exhibits focused on the earth's history from the beginning of creation and included animatronic dinosaurs, talking heroes of the Bible, and many displays that honored God's Word. It is an enormous, inspiring and educational facility. When we boarded the bus several hours later after absorbing many visual and audio treats, a surprise awaited us.

My husband had shared with someone on the bus that he had begun an amateur singing career after retiring several years ago from veterinary medicine at the University of

Georgia. A few minutes after we headed to the hotel for the night, he was recruited to sing one of the songs in his repertoire. Microphone in hand (which had been used previously only by the bus driver and tour leader to provide information about the daily schedule, give instructions pertaining to each stop, and reprimands for not listening to the announcements), Larry sang "One Pair of Hands." This gorgeous song describes how God created the world, quieted storms, healed the sick and raised the dead, and then encourages everyone who hears this testimony to put their faith into "One Pair of Hands." Our group had enjoyed singing songs, laughing, eating a lot of snacks, and watching movies. Now, worship was ringing throughout the bus. Jesus was making Himself known in those spontaneous moments. We knew He was there all along, but now we were more aware of His presence. Larry was meant to be on that bus. We all were.

On our third day of the trip, we arrived at the Ark Encounter. I had seen videos and pictures of this marvel, but was astounded at the massive size. Every time I read about the dimensions of the ark in the Bible, I tried unsuccessfully to visualize it. Describing its length in terms of how many buses or football fields does not do it for me! I was blown over when I saw this virtual portrayal of the ark for the first time. It is huge!

Among the exhibits on the ark was a "talking Noah" who seemed almost lifelike. Noah lived to be 600 years old, and he needed a very long life to complete what God had assigned him to do. It is believed that it took 100 years for Him to build the ark. Noah's staggering beautiful testimony of obedience, in a time when rain had never before fallen on the earth, has touched the lives of millions of believers. How much taunting did Noah receive in the midst of a disbelieving, evil world? It didn't matter, because it was God's voice that spoke the loudest to him. It was a tremendous blessing to see this portrayal of the ark firsthand. It is truly an inspiring representation of a majestic accomplishment by God through a prophet's hands!

As I sat outside the ark that afternoon, I chatted up a woman from our group whom I had not known before. We were able to use each other's first names in friendly conversation, because our very organized leader had given us name tags the first day of the trip. This lady looked at my name and asked me if I had taught at a particular middle school in our community back home. When I told her I had, she said that she recognized my name and that her son frequently spoke fondly of me. He had been my student over thirty years ago! How sweet of Jesus to put us together, side by side in that moment. That was not a coincidence! That is what I call a God Postmark, a sign that He was in the midst of my encounter at the ark that day. Jesus loves to bless people with a common *thread* by putting them side by side in all kinds of situations. It is one of His "specialties."

That last night on the trip we stayed at the Shaker Village in Pleasant Hill, Kentucky. The buildings in this community were built over two hundred years ago and had been restored in the 1960s to look again like they did in the 19th century. The stories of the devout Shakers seemed to be "baked" into the rooms. I felt a kindred spirit with these people, who had passed from this earth a very long time ago, because they also searched for ways to be closer to God. To see some of the things memorialized in the Bible certainly accomplished that for me. The Shakers and our tour group had been on the same journey in different ways and in different periods of time. God found a way to synchronize us. He does that throughout time, no matter how many hundreds of years separate us.

Before I left on this four-day bus trip, I had anticipated finding great inspiration in the two Christian tourist attractions on my bucket list. Amazingly, God bestowed on me many more blessings than I could have foreseen. He gave me an awareness of His smoothing out of rough places, providing connections with strangers, and responding to our prayer requests. It was definitely a trip worth taking. I will never forget it.

Look at the rough places in your life, the unexpected en-counters with strangers, and the prayers spoken aloud in a difficult situation. Jesus is right there beside you, whispering in your ear, "I will take care of you and give you a new vision for the path you are traveling. Look at your ashes and see the beauty I make from them." Remember, you have to look. The beauty is there.

Larry and I (He was a trooper!)

I think this is the horse that bites!

Horse for Jesus to ride?

God Himself closed the door!

Genesis 7:13-17

"On that very day Noah and his sons, Shem, Ham and Japheth, together with his wife and the wives of his three sons, entered the ark. They had with them every wild animal according to its kind, all livestock according to their kinds, every creature that moves along the ground according to its kind, everything with wings. Pairs of all creatures that have the breath of life in them came to Noah and entered the ark. The animals going in were male and female of every living thing, as God commanded Noah.

Then the LORD shut him in."

<u>Luke 19:1-10</u>

He entered Jericho and was passing through. And behold there was a man named Zacchaeus. He was a chief tax collector and was rich. And he was seeking to see who Jesus was, but on account of the crowd he could not, because he was short in stature. So, he ran ahead and climbed up into a sycamore tree to see him, for he was about to pass that way. And when Jesus came to the place, he looked up and said to him, "Zacchaeus, hurry and come down, for I must stay at your house today.

So he hurried down and received him joyfully. And when they saw it, they all grumbled. "He has gone in to be the guest of a man who is a sinner." And Zacchaeus stood and said to the Lord," Behold, Lord, the half of my goods I give to the poor. And if I have defrauded anyone of anything, I restore it fourfold." And Jesus said to him, "Today salvation has come to this house, since he also is a son of Abraham. For the Son of Man came to seek and to save the lost."

Chapter Eleven

Jesus and Zacchaeus in my Classroom

I was constantly aware of him when he was in my middle school science classroom. His challenging behavior required a lot of my attention and daily prayers about our time together. I certainly wasn't capable of successfully navigating this kind of turbulence with my own strength. I knew it had to be accomplished in a way that created a positive atmosphere not only for him, but for all the other students. I felt like the Lord had purposely placed him with me, and that belief inspired me to persevere throughout the year. Remembering this special young man thirty years later, I cherish the gift he was to me. This thirteen-year-old student's name will remain a secret, and so I will just call him Zacchaeus.

The story of Zacchaeus and Jesus in the New Testament is one of my favorites. They were a surprising twosome, because Zacchaeus was a corrupt tax collector and Jesus was the Son of God. Our Lord could see the promise in the soul of this man who was an outcast in his community. Actually, He loved hanging out with people who were on the outskirts of society. Perhaps it was because He could see the emptiness and hunger inside of them which the world could not satisfy. Jesus could always see what others could not. He saw Zacchaeus climb into a tree so he could get a better view of Him, whereas some who stood right in front of Jesus had no hunger whatsoever to recognize Him.

Jesus always has a set of *special lenses* for us, so we can see in others what the world cannot. He frequently gave me opportunities with "disruptive" students to recognize their potential which lay hidden beneath their difficult behavior. Most of them seemed to like me and joyfully participated in my science classes. However, the rapport I had with them did not eliminate their impulsive behavior during my instruction. It did enable me to observe the Lord at work. I could witness Him transform frustrations into revelations. The joy from success came and replaced the misery of failure.

My Zacchaeus was well known to all the teachers in the school. Disruption was his specialty, yet he was perfectly placed with me. During each summer vacation I asked God to oversee the placement of students assigned to me and heal any brokenness in them. I wanted every child—quiet, rambunctious, highly intellectual, challenged in cognitive skills, depressed or gregarious—to be touched by Him when they were in my classroom. I prayed that He would reveal Himself to them through my hands-on science activities. Being prohibited to openly speak about our Lord was not a limitation. When Jesus' spirit is inside believers, He always makes Himself known. He was always in my classroom.

I quickly learned that although Zacchaeus struggled with written assignments and tests, he excelled with hands-on pursuits in electricity, sound energy, light energy, chemistry, and in other physical science topics. His face would light up upon successfully completing a task, and frequently he was even able to assist others. What his mind could not read and interpret, his hands could as he held materials that focused on the concept to be learned. When I was able to keep him attentive to the positive opportunities in front of him, the verbal, destructive interruptions did not occur. This resulted in both of us having a day where we could smile and sometimes even laugh together. Laughter soothed out many rough places with him.

Laughter is one of the most powerful sounds heard in a classroom. A sense of humor is a wonderful quality for teachers to have. I believe it made a difference for me with not only students like Zacchaeus, but also with all my students. I stumbled upon its potency when I first began my teaching career. One of my students who was very displeased with me decided to draw a witch and label it "Mrs. Cornelius." When

I discovered her artwork, I mischievously said, "I look great!" The young lady was pretty surprised with my response, and we laughed together. Spectacular grace comes many times through unanticipated laughter.

I am sure Jesus laughed with my Zacchaeus and me on several occasions. Sometimes, this young man would test me with offhand comments just to get a reaction, and I would respond with humor. One day, he said, "Mrs. C, you are crazy!" My response was, "It is a requirement for this job." We both laughed. Diffusing a situation with inspired humor is powerful. I call it "spiritual oxygen." I can just see this happening with Jesus and His Zacchaeus. Those moments of witnessing discord turned away empty- handed are "heaven sent."

Many "heaven sent" resources are given to us when we have a divine assignment, and sometimes that includes a special person. God loves to put people together who are synchronized with His purpose. At the beginning of my school year with Zacchaeus, I was given a dedicated partner who was a behavior specialist at the school. We met frequently in our quest to discover methods for helping him navigate through his behavioral and academic challenges. The two of us were committed to making him successful at school, and our shared devotion generated a great friendship between us.

We prayerfully pursued ways we could achieve our goals that were uniquely suited to him. We created behavior modification check lists to motivate him to find his *power* in positive ways, instead of negative ones. Our plan specified that after earning a certain number of points, he could select one of three rewards. Zacchaeus's choices caused me to see Jesus's sense of humor. This child who brought so much stress to my life frequently chose to be with <u>me</u> in the afterschool hours. My Zacchaeus was not too different from the one Jesus encountered. Mine did not have to climb up a tree to see me, but he definitely liked having one-on-one time with me

On one particular occasion, my prized student earned enough points for me to take him to the Dairy Queen for an ice cream cone. As I sat there with him, enjoying a sweet conversation, I could see a very happy face. That moment was a testimony of Jesus at work in both of us—away from a structured environment.

Some of Zaccheus's challenges which affected his behavior were physical in nature. He had an abnormal duplication of four upper front teeth. The baby teeth had not fallen out and the permanent teeth came in behind them. This gave him an unusual appearance which resulted in a lot of teasing from other students.

I began to wonder, "What if a visit to a dentist to correct this problem changed his life?" My partner and I decided we had to find a way to make that happen. We then approached his parents about having a dental procedure done. We were not surprised to learn that they had no insurance to cover the cost, but when we were able to secure private funding for the procedure, they readily agreed to have it done. Honestly today, I might be concerned about a lawsuit in doing this. Thirty years ago, I lived in a time of grace where I could safely proceed. I also know that if I had this same student in my care today, the Lord would provide other opportunities for it to be accomplished.

I don't know what happened to my Zacchaeus, because I didn't see him after he left middle school. The Lord never again put him in my path, but I believe my obedience to what He had called me to do touched both of our lives with eternal significance. I am confident that this child's life was imprinted by God in ways that followed him into adulthood, and I will never forget experiencing God's presence when I was with him. Zacchaeus was a gift.

Perhaps there is a kind of beauty to be savored in not knowing the rest of the story with this child. Sometimes, what we experience in walking in obedience with the Lord is the treasure all by itself. I taught a few thousand children over more than thirty years of teaching, and I was blessed to see Jesus at work in the lives of many of them. He taught me that He could make a difference through me, and that revelation gave me purpose and fulfillment that will always be with me.

Many times, it takes only one person to impact some-one's life in a way that leads to their recognizing God's path for them. When that path is then traveled, it is not just their life that is blessed, but that of many, many others whom they touch. The opportunities the Lord provides for this to hap-pen can come anywhere and anytime. The opportunity may come in a classroom setting, in a workplace environment, in a hospital waiting room, or even with a stressed-out stranger standing in a long checkout line in a busy store.

Jesus can be very powerful in any of these situations, if we let him. If adversity is also present, He can bring about spectacular results through you. He can transform your diffi-cult encounters into ones where His presence is felt, and you will receive the gift of being by His side. Watch him make something beautiful out of those opportunities.

Jesus still reaches out to others in all situations.

* Grandsons Jeffrey Cornelius and Robert Cornelius role playing Zacchaeus.

<u>2 Corinthians 1: 3-7</u>

All praise to the God and Father of our Lord Jesus Christ. He is the source of every mercy and the God who comforts us. He comforts us in all our troubles so that we can comfort others. When others are troubled, we will be able to give them the same comfort God has given us. You can be sure that the more we suffer for Christ, the more God will shower us with his comfort through Christ.

Chapter Twelve

Comfort Released from Ashes of Sorrow

The seven-year-old girl stood in her neighbor's guest bedroom and overheard the words of her Aunt Betty," He died last night." Her aunt had just arrived at the front door to share the sad news with Mrs. Cress. The little girl had been sent across the street to spend the night with this neighbor who had always been regarded as a member of the family. The devastating message penetrated the child's heart so deeply, that she would still be able to hear it seventy years later. She was the sister of the dead child. Bobby had died during the night as his mother, father, uncle and aunt watched him go.

Mrs. Cress considered Bobby to be her grandchild. He once requested a motorized Erecter Ferris Wheel for Christmas, and she had gladly purchased it only to have it destroyed when she was in a car accident on her way home. Only slightly injured, she went back the next day to buy a new one. She was not going to let anything keep her from getting that toy for this child.

The little girl also loved her brother. She had felt so special when she was able to be with him at school one day when he was in first grade. This was the only year of school that his health would allow him to experience. On rare occasions, children in his class were allowed to bring a sibling to class. On that day Bobby demonstrated how his unique folding cup expanded to full size. It was in his lunch box, and he could use it to get water at meal time. His little sister was very impressed with his cup and getting to be with him at school. The two of them were a sweet twosome.

Many, many prayers were spoken for Bobby over the three years that his health slowly deteriorated. His parents had been told a few months before his passing that the end was near. They, as well as their circle of friends, rejected the prognosis. Pastors of local churches came to their home and prayed for God to intervene and save his life. His little sister prayed every night before she went to bed, "God, please heal my brother Bobby."

Did God not hear the little sister's prayers? Did He not hear the hundreds of prayers from others in the community? His mother, who was a nurse, and his father, who was a high school teacher, were very respected and loved by many. They had a huge circle of friends who were hoping and praying for a miracle for their son. Yet, Robert Dale Spencer left this earth in 1952 a few weeks before his tenth birthday.

I vividly remember the heartache of his passing because I was the little girl who heard the words, "He died last night." As I write them today, they still feel like knives piercing my heart. For a few years after Bobby's death, I dreamed about the loss of my brother. In my dreams he was simply missing in the house, and I frantically searched for him in every room. Was he in the toy box? Surely, if I kept looking, I would find him. Then, I would awaken. I would have that same dream, over and over.

I have missed Bobby throughout my long life. Yet, in a way, I have never been without my older brother. My memories of him have always been with me. The aching loss of him, and the profound sorrow that invaded our home when he died, was framed in hope and not disbelief. My parents' faith remained strong because they believed that Bobby was *not* gone forever and was waiting for them in heaven. The pain of his death created a deep-seated need in me to console others who were struggling. The ability to do that produces a healing salve for my hurting spirit. When anyone speaks of a child who has died, I have heartfelt sympathy to extend to them.

Bobby was joined by my father over forty years ago, and by my mother just a few years ago. I saw my parents tirelessly pour themselves into the lives of others. They were able to offer comfort which originated from the place where their great heartache resided. Doing that also softened their pain.

My father frequently spoke to me about how his loss made him very compassionate with his high school students. His desire to meet their needs intensified after his tragedy of losing his only son. He would ask them: "Do you need lunch money? Do you need extra tutoring to pass your classes?" He quickly offered words of encouragement when their personal lives spelled out disaster.

Blessing the lives of others rewarded him with "healing balm" for his own spirit. When one of my former high school classmates lost her youngest son who was four, he was there to cry with her and her husband. Because my father had walked the same road of sorrow, he knew words that would console them. There in the agony of someone else's loss, love from shared sorrow was beautifully manifested.

My mother, who was an obstetrics nurse, felt the same way when she cared for her patients. She felt that her work encompassed more than a professional obligation; she wanted God to use her to contribute to the new parents' and their babies' lives. This caring attitude was not only a part of her hours as a nurse, but continued on in her personal life. I will never forget the occasion when she stayed up all night with a dying friend, and then went to work the next day without sleep. Pain as deep and penetrating as hers and my father's needed to experience the relief that can only come from comforting others.

My brother did not have the miracle that was desperately desired on this side of eternity, but God gave another one in its place. I witnessed my parents' courage and faith as they grieved. This made an indelible imprint on the way I faced the heartaches in my own life.

I saw how their heartbreak sensitized them to the emotional pain of others and gave them a burning need to offer relief. I wanted to replicate in my own life what they had modeled. I spent over thirty years teaching middle school math and science, and I was always drawn to the students who were the most vulnerable. If I could identify a teaching technique that matched their learning style and helped them to succeed, I knew I was fulfilling the ministry God had given me. Nurturing my students softened the pain I experienced as a child when my brother died. The agony of my sorrow dimmed as my love for the children in my classroom was manifested.

Grief that resides in the crevices of our souls can be flushed out with love. As we pour love into the lives of others who are suffering, a healing salve is released in us. We begin to have less and less room for sorrow. The power grief has over our daily lives then begins to diminish slowly, but continually.

Who do you know who has had a tragedy in their lives and decided to live to bless others? Can you see people in your life who need someone to do this for them? Could you be that person? Ask God to transform your ashes of grief into something that will bring light and beauty into the lives of others.

Psalm 27:10

Even if my father and mother abandon me, the LORD will hold me close.

Psalm 34:18

The LORD is close to the brokenhearted; he rescues those whose spirits are crushed.

John 14:16

I will pray to the Father, and he shall give you another Comforter, that he may abide with you forever.

Chapter Thirteen

Mr. Comfort Bear

He arrived in a gift box sent by my close friend Robin. It was my birthday and this was a special present from her. He was a small teddy bear, who although purchased new in a local store, had the appearance of being decades old and worn out by loving hands. Robin and I have been exchanging birthday and Christmas gifts for many years, and she always manages to find thoughtful, unique items to fulfill needs I was yet to identify.

He looked like the way I felt some days in my middle school classroom—a little frazzled. Just looking at him made me smile. Who could have known that a new-*used looking* bear had the capability to fill a void in me? Perhaps the vendor knew there were many sentimental people in the world who wished they could still hold their childhood teddy bear. Then again, some might not have had the memory of experiencing solace in that way, but wished they did.

Despite your age, you always want someone or something to soothe your aching spirit. I think about the sadness I experienced as a young child when my brother, after being bedridden for three years, passed away. I also remember the disruptive homelife some of my friends experienced when they were growing up. At times, having something soft to hold even if it is just a stuffed animal, alleviates some emotional pain.

After I had enjoyed my bear for a few years, I placed a large nametag on him, Mr. Comfort Bear. I then loaned him to

99

a teacher friend who was having a challenging day. This was the beginning of my bear having several journeys with others and then being intermittently returned to me. Underneath his name, a description of his travels was recorded for everyone to enjoy. Once, he disappeared for several months, and then it was discovered someone had taken him to his father in a nursing home. Somehow, (with a little help from a human), Mr. Comfort Bear found his way back to me. Amazingly, this routine continued for over fifteen years, until I gave him a permanent home with one of my friends whose husband had died. Who knew that adults could relate to a stuffed animal in a way that could soothe their spirits?

The Overstreets, who were on my mother's side of the family, believed this to be true. No fooling them about adults sometimes being childlike in their inner selves. These relatives were loving and creative in ways that I always admired and wished to emulate. They were expert huggers, and no matter your age, they always made you feel like you were a beloved child. I had one special uncle, Aaron Overstreet, who frequently gave me "bear" hugs, even after I had transitioned to middle age.

A member of the Overstreet family began the custom of sending small teddy bears instead of flowers to friends and relatives who were ill. No dead flowers to later have to throw away! The stuffed bears remained to give comfort even after the recipients healed. Trash cans were not the forever home for these appealing gifts.

The charm of teddy bears began over a hundred years ago when they were named after President Teddy Roosevelt. Perhaps they have remained popular because they make people feel like a cherished child in an unwelcoming world. Some of us who grew up in the 1950s and 1960s have loving memories of an era when the world seemed more innocent. We have recollections from this period of time about favorite children's books, Walt Disney characters and, cheerful movies. Possibly, people throughout the decades have felt this same kind of nostalgia. In the last thirty years computers, cell phones, and the internet have decreased opportunities for social interaction. For some people this creates an empty void, and possibly having a teddy bear helps them feel less lonely.

Occasionally, some of the iconic stuffed animals with special "powers" have been found in anointed places of worship. The congregation of Sky Valley Chapel in Sky Valley,

Georgia has for many years lovingly placed teddy bears in some of their pews. Each one dressed in a special handmade outfit has an attached message which certifies the bear has been in a place of worship, heard prayers, and witnessed songs of worship being offered to God. Visitors were invited to give the bears a new home with someone needing encouragement. Who would not be blessed by receiving one of those bears?

Some time ago, after visiting Sky Valley Chapel, I took one of their bears to a dear friend who was having a serious health crisis. After recovering, she gave it to her ten-year-old grandson Tristan, who was ill at the time. He remarked when he held it, "It feels so soft!" These words brought tears to the eyes of his family, because they had heard him speak the very same words after a tragedy. He was only seven years old when he and his father were in a horrific car crash.

They survived, but the friend who was driving perished. Although Tristan's father was seriously injured, this little boy who had been in the back seat of the car, escaped without even a scratch. Shortly after the accident, Tristan told his grandmother, "The angel's wings were so soft!" He sweetly remembered the angel's deliverance when he held the cuddly bear.

Possibly, a young boy's experience of feeling comfort when holding something soft is what others sense when they connect to a past memory of being cared for and loved. Perhaps, for them it unknowingly simulates being held by an angel. Wouldn't it be wonderful if this sensation could be given to others through the arms of human "angels?" Maybe it can through you.

God knows how much we need to be held and loved, and He gives us an invincible way to experience this. He places His very own spirit inside of us, so we can feel the soft presence of His embrace. The Holy Spirit is our comforter, and He can empower us to perceive the heartaches of others and respond in a way that softens their pain.

When we comfort others as we have been comforted by the Lord, He takes the ashes of emotional pain and transforms them into a beautiful exchange of love between two people. Because His spirit rests inside of us, every time we hug someone, it is God doing the hugging.

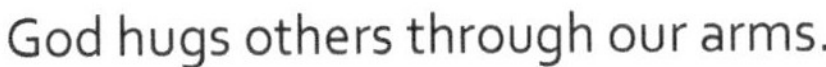

God hugs others through our arms.

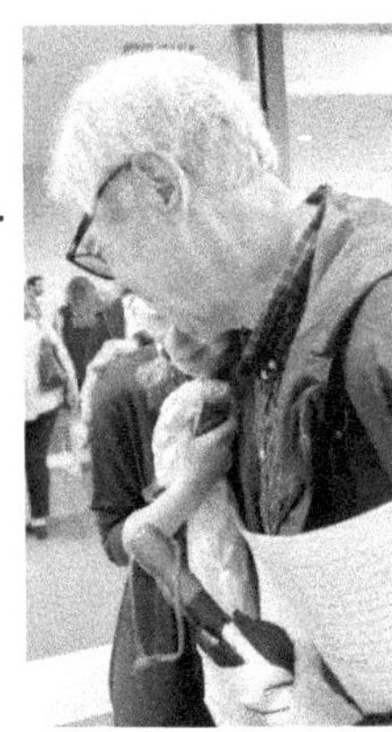

<u>James 1:2-4</u>

Consider it pure joy, my brothers and sisters, whenever you face trials of many kinds, because you know that the testing of your faith produces perseverance. Let perseverance finish its work so that you may be mature and complete, not lacking anything.

Chapter Fourteen
Windows of Grace

I was having one of those days! You know the kind, where obstacles present themselves in groups of three. A road crew had unexpectantly shown up that morning to resurface the asphalt in my cul-de-sac and the adjacent street. No one in the neighborhood had been alerted about this gift of re-paved roads. I realized that in a couple of hours, I might have trouble exiting my driveway to meet my daughter and her three children for lunch. Yet, when the time came to leave, I was able to successfully maneuver my red convertible around several workers and their road equipment to happily embrace the day! My moment of celebration was short-lived. I soon faced another obstacle as I neared the entrance to my subdivision. Several self-absorbed geese appeared and began walking slowly, slowly, slowly across the road right in front of my car. No quick departure for me!

Despite my adventures with the road crew and the geese, I arrived early at IHOP and parked. I then decided to lower the windows and wait a few minutes before going into the restaurant. I had no reason to anticipate another challenge, but I was in for a big surprise! When I realized it was time to go in, I tried restarting the car so I could raise the windows. I then heard a terrible clicking noise. A feeling of dread swept over me as I remembered this unpleasant sound from some previous experiences with other vehicles. I tried a few more times to coax the ignition into working. Why is it that one has a futile need to keep trying to get a dead battery to recharge itself, before reason takes over? I think it is the "keep pushing the button syndrome" that occurs when you wait impatiently for an elevator. I knew I was not going to leave anytime soon after finishing lunch. I had a *deceased* battery.

Later, after having a delightful meal with my family, the battery was given temporary "life" at the restaurant by one of God's human angels who just happened to have jumper cables. I was then able to leave IHOP and go to the dealership to purchase a new one. No road crew there. No geese there. Instead, upon arriving I noticed a long, long line to be checked in by a service technician. This situation was created because one of their door's malfunctioning had eliminated their ability to have a second line. When two lines are open, the vehicles quickly move to the garage entrance. (I just think the door knew I was coming.)

Sounds like a frustrating day? Not really. Windows of grace opened at each juncture. That morning when I first observed the road crew setting up in front of my house, I went out to greet them. It seemed like a good time to thank them for providing a new road, especially with the weather forecast of a temperature in the nineties that day. I then asked about being able to leave my driveway in a couple of hours, and was rewarded with the response," You will have no problem. We will help you."

Later, when I was ready to depart, one of the men moved his service vehicle which was blocking my path, and the driver of the large truck spitting out asphalt shut it down temporarily to let me pass by. That was God's favor in the midst of a broken road being made new!

While I was at IHOP with the dead battery, my eldest granddaughter (she was my "human angel") who had arrived before me, informed me that she had jumper cables in her car. Unlike me, she knew how to use them! (She's always been smarter and more mature than me.) All we had to do was go ahead into the restaurant and as we enjoyed our lunch, watch the parking lot. We decided that, when the vehicle next to mine left, my granddaughter would quickly move her car into the parking space. The trick was to get there fast enough before another vehicle arrived in the crowded parking lot.

When we later spotted the vehicle leaving, we went "flying" out of the restaurant. I forgot to put my napkin down, and I was unintentionally using it like a white flag at a race. Now, don't you think that created a few giggles? I am pretty sure our waitress had probably witnessed this, because we had a very jolly conversation with her when she first came to our table. She knew who she was dealing with for sure! Her joy when she took our order was definitely a sign of God's favor.

After my granddaughter had successfully rejuvenated my battery, a man came over from the car wash next door to see if he could help. Upon arriving, he could see that everything was in hand. He remarked, "I saw a young woman and her grandmother needing assistance, but now I see everything is finished. This is the first time I have ever seen a young girl know how to recharge a battery!" I proudly told my granddaughter, Alyssa, "It was worth getting a dead battery just to see you take charge and rescue me." Hearing the astonished remarks of a stranger, made it all the sweeter for me.

Now, about the long line at the dealership. It moved more quickly than my brain anticipated (two years or more?). I waited patiently in the customer lounge for just over an hour or two. During that time, I was treated to one of those shows on television where people have to choose between purchasing a new home or keeping the one that had been remodeled for them. I had been known in previous visits to not leave immediately after being informed my vehicle was ready because I wanted to see what the homeowners decided. I am fascinated with remodeling stuff, and I always returned home with creative visions for remodeling my home. (To my husband's relief, those grand ideas evaporated quickly.)

Not only did I enjoy the television program, I also had a book with me for another source of entertainment. I have had a habit for many years to never go anywhere without reading material in case I find myself in a situation that requires me to wait. I read several inspiring chapters about the character of God in my "bonus time." Even though the book didn't mention it, I am very sure He has an awesome sense of humor. My day was supporting that belief.

So, bottom line, I was totally entertained in very unexpected ways by the obstacles that came my way (even the geese). I saw God turn the ashes of my circumstances into unexpected delights. I couldn't help thanking Him that day by saying, "Heavenly Father, You rocked my world! I saw You take my potential stress and turn it inside out to reveal nuggets of joy!" Actually, joy "sneaked up" on me all day. I love it when God does that!

God opens windows of grace every day for us, and we sometimes decide to shut them and forfeit His gift. Frequently, He uses adversity to expand our horizons about the world, and give us opportunities to demonstrate we belong to Him.

He plants people all around us so we can receive the blessings of His undeserved favor. He also gives us the same opportunity to do that for people who are struggling in a hurting world. The world needs more smiles, joy, and grace. You can be the multiplier of these and call forth God's kingdom in the midst of surprising circumstances. Doing this might surprise the world with refreshing ways to view struggles. It might even become contagious in the best way possible!

Philippians 4:6-7

Don't worry about anything: instead, pray about everything. Tell God what you need, and thank him for all he has done. Then you will experience God's peace, which exceeds anything we understand. His peace will guard your hearts and minds as you live in Christ Jesus.

Chapter Fifteen
Jesus at the Gas Pump

It is said that Jesus is everywhere, but at the gas pump? Really? Well, I am pretty sure He hung out there a few years ago when I met up with a friend. I had recently noticed that Chris and his wife Susan had not been at the 11:00 church service for several weeks. Since we had two different services, traditional and contemporary, I speculated they were now going to the other one. Unfortunately, I hadn't called to check and tell them I had missed them.

For some time, I had had a special connection with them. Chris and I shared a powerful prayer history. Over twenty years ago, some of us in a Bible study joined him in the intensive care unit at our local hospital to pray for a friend in our group who had recently had a kidney transplant and due to complications was in critical condition. Since we were not allowed to enter her room, we stood in the hallway and placed our hands on the door. We prayed for healing and a testimony to share with the world. Sometimes when we boldly approach God to ask for a miraculous healing, He says, no. This time God said yes. He gave her the immeasurable gift of being able to raise two young sons to adulthood and see them have their own children. She is today reveling in being a grandmother and continues to lift up her voice to God in praise and thanksgiving. I will forever remember those moments of praying with Chris and the others in the hospital. We felt Jesus was there with us in the hallway, standing right beside us.

Chris believes that God can make the impossible, possible, and he is always going to ask for the miracle. Spending time with a man like him makes his faith *contagious*. Everyone should be "contaminated" by him. Over fifteen years ago some of us who were in a Bible study with Chris partnered with him to pray that he and his wife would be able to adopt a baby from China.

It looked for some time that the dream Chris and Susan had of becoming parents was not going to happen. Chris spurred everyone on with his vision of his future daughter. He kept saying, "I can see her in my arms."

After many twists and turns and valleys of discouragement, they finally became parents of a baby girl. When they returned from China, someone took a picture of her in Chris's arms at the airport. What he had seen in his vision had now come to fruition. God came through in a magnificent, thrilling way. Returning home from their very long trip, they put their precious child in a baby bed which had been *waiting* three years for her. It had been a symbol of their faith, but now was a representation of a glorious answer to prayer.

Even though it had been many years since this miracle, I always think about it when I see Chris. I'm so happy I didn't miss seeing him that day at the gas station. I have been accused many times of having my "head in the clouds. People tell me all the time that they saw me on the road and honked at me without any recognition or response. I tell them that they should be grateful that this one "distracted lady" is watching the road. Fortunately, Chris saw me first.

With a huge smile on his face, he ran over to talk to me. I quickly told him I had not seen him and Susan at church for a while, and then I casually asked if everything was all right. He was very open with his answer and shared that his family had been visiting other churches. The conversation then became very personal when he shared the news that he had recently been diagnosed with cancer. His surgery was only two weeks away.

Chris asked me to keep him in my prayers. I immediately stopped and placed my hand on his, and asked if I could pray for him right then. He quickly said yes. No need to worry about being at a gas station with others around to listen. The spirit of Jesus poured out on us, right next to the gas pumps. God answered our prayer and today Chris is cancer free.

We met Jesus together in the place and time God had provided. There are no accidental meetings with our Lord. There are opportunities from Him all the time and nudging from His spirit to prompt us. I asked Chris if he would like our pastor to come pray with him, and he quickly said yes. She then was able to be there at the hospital with him before the surgery.

Our paster would not have known about the surgery if the Lord had not put Chris and me together. Both of us deciding we needed to fill our gas tanks at the same location, day, and time was not a coincidence. It was another God "postmark" to show us that He is with us wherever we are, even at gas stations.

Look for people in your midst who may need more than a casual conversation. Listen to a prompting in your spirit, and put busyness aside to be Jesus to them. Focus on the person and inquire about how their life is unfolding that day. Instead of asking how they are, ask if there is anything you can pray about for them. Be bold and do it then and there. Prayers for them later on may not happen because of all the world's distractions. Grasp the opportunity in front of you, and watch Jesus make ashes into beauty for that person. It will happen not just for them, but also for you.

<u>Luke 15: 8-10</u>

"Or what woman, having ten silver coins does not light a lamp, sweep the house, and search carefully until she finds it? And when she has found it, she calls her friends and neighbors together, saying, 'Rejoice with me, for I have found the piece Which I lost."

Chapter Sixteen
The Lost Christmas Gift

There it was, under the bench in our dining room. It was in a medium-sized dark maroon gift bag, hidden from sight after I placed it there during the Christmas rush. With the numerous wrapped gifts under the nearby Christmas tree, there was scant space for one already unwrapped. I had always placed opened presents under the tree as a reminder to acknowledge them later with thoughtful thank you notes. Not only am I extremely slow about writing these notes, I have also needed the visual prompting of the gifts as reminders. Pitiful, I know. I am really good at pitiful. At least I recognize my condition.

After my husband had opened this present, a couple of days before Christmas, I hastily pushed it under a small bench. There it stayed for several weeks. The abandoned bag held three items my husband's best friend had given him—a golf ball marker, a golf coffee cup, and most thoughtful of all, an autographed book from a local author he really enjoyed.

Forgetting the value of its contents, Larry and I both lost all memory of the gift. Had I been a meticulous housekeeper and more organized, we might have been saved from this predicament. (Frankly, I believe several creative geniuses in the world have been described as having the same problem and lost some of their stuff! I understand Albert Einstein had a messy desk).

Two weeks after Christmas, my husband's friend asked how he liked his gifts. Having forgotten receiving them, we knew we needed to admit they had been misplaced. To make matters worse, we would also have to confess that we didn't even remember what they were. It is impossible to write a coherent, deeply felt note of appreciation in this kind of situation, and so we had no choice but face our embarrassment. Thus, we confessed our callous treatment of his inspired and generous gift giving.

Actually, there was no *we*, it was <u>just me</u>. My husband, with some relief, told his friend that it was my doing. I was very happy to take the blame. This felt better than confirmation I was losing my mind! (I had come up with all kinds of improbable scenarios to explain the mystery of the missing present!)

Misplacing important things is not a new experience for me. As an example, I have been known for many years as a" chocoholic." This occasionally has led me to conduct frantic searches in my kitchen cabinets for chocolate. I must have this "drug" and then of course there is my other drug, caffeine. I need my daily dose of chocolate and my morning coffee, or those closet to me are at risk of *not* receiving much grace! (On the other hand, I need a gigantic supply of grace from others.) Just get out of my way when I can't readily find coffee and chocolate.

However, there are some fringe benefits to misplacing important items. I accomplish a great deal of reorganizing, and discover long-forgotten items. My disorganized drawers and closets experience a "revival" when I conduct my obsessive searches. I recognize many things that need to find a new home in the trash can. Yes, I save the good stuff for thrift shops, Salvation Army, etc. They receive these *treasures* even though they might have difficulty getting someone to buy them. I have seen dumpsters located close to their stores which is a very convenient place for donations not wanted by any living soul. After clearing out a lot of stuff, I am able to see what I can really use. These treasures had simply disappeared in all the chaos of the vast clutter around them.

It really is not totally my fault that things get out of hand. Objects placed behind closed doors and in busy drawers just multiply on their own. Now if you think I am unnecessarily personifying non-living objects, let me remind you that when you put coffee cups in your cabinet and close the door, it seems like they "breed." Ever throw them away because of no room, only to be in the same predicament a few weeks later?

As I sit here laughing at myself, I feel absolutely no remorse for the mismanagement of my stuff. I began using myself as a subject for humor a few years ago. I wish I had learned this fifty years ago. Life has been so much enjoyable since I acquired this new talent and began to realize where I should expend my emotional energy!

All humor aside, Larry and I felt tremendous relief when I found the gift bag. He was then able to write an appropriate and caring thank you note to his forgiving friend. I then began to ponder: "What if I spent some of the time, money, and priority I have used for material pursuits on spiritual ones instead? After all, one item I display every Christmas is a plaque with the words: "Jesus is the gift." I see many Christmas celebrations around the world that seem to have forgotten their original purpose: commemorating the birth of our Savior who came to rescue us from eternal death. I sometimes see this lapse happening with people I know and love, and I most clearly see it when it happens to me. Let us not lose sight of the the most precious gift the world has ever seen.

Jesus is the Christmas gift we can receive every day. We seem to lose Him when we push Him under a "bench" made of distractions: technology gadgets, television, watching movies, shopping, texting, etc. This list is long and it gets longer every day. Clear your mind and heart of all the clutter, and see the "ashes" of your situation turn into some beautiful time with the Lord. Don't lose this gift. It has eternal value.

JESUS

1 Corinthians 13:4-8a

Love is patient, love is kind. It does not envy, it does not boast, it is not proud. It is not rude, it is not self-seeking, it is not easily angered, it keeps no record of wrongs. Love does not delight in evil but rejoices with truth. It always protects, always trusts, always hopes, always perseveres.

Love never fails.

1 Corinthians 15:42-45

So will it be with the resurrection of the dead. The body that is sown is perishable, it is raised imperishable. It is sown in dishonor, it is raised in glory; It is sown in weakness, it is raised in power; it is sown a natural body, it is raised a spiritual body.

Chapter Seventeen
A Lifetime of Love

I remember the first time I held his hand. I was eighteen and he was about to be twenty. We were on our first date, and when we walked across the street, his hand reached for mine. We were at Purdue University where he was a student, and I was on spring break from Indiana University. Sixty years later, after he had suffered several years of diminished health, I held his hand for the last time as he lay dying. During our time together God wove a beautiful story for us which included almost fifty-seven years of marriage.

If there is such a thing as love at first sight (and I believe there is), Larry and I experienced it when we first met. I was with my cousin Mary Dell at a bowling alley on the Purdue campus. She lived in a female cooperative house where students lived like a family and shared housekeeping, cooking, and other chores. Her co-op house was competing against a male co-op house in a bowling match, but only she and two housemates were available that day. She couldn't find a fourth person, and since I had been visiting with her, I very reluctantly became the substitute. I had no idea how blessed I would be from that decision. I vividly remember at some point spontaneously sitting next to Larry at the bowling alley and chatting away! I was feeling very outgoing that day.

Later after my cousin and I had returned to her house, I received a call from Larry inviting me for a Coke date. (Coke was just a soft drink beverage in those days.) I remember say-ing, "I would love to!" Many decades later I learned he ini-tially thought I was also a Purdue student, but thankfully his learning I lived a hundred miles away at Indiana University did not deter him. At the end of that first date, we exchanged addresses, with mine written on a tiny piece of scrap paper. Just a few years ago, he showed me he still had this now yel-lowed address in his wallet. He had kept it all this time. I was honestly very surprised by his sentimentality, because I always thought I was the one who was most nostalgic! This treasured memento is currently placed in my memory box, along with some of the loving cards Larry gave me through-out the years.

Almost three years after that first date, a week before Christmas, we were married in my small church in Carbon, Indiana (population of five hundred at the time). We were very young when we began planning our wedding, and as we were still both students, we had to wait until I graduated. I could then support us as an elementary school teacher during his last year of college in Veterinary Medicine. To mark our time, I made a "wedding calendar" for Larry that was simi-lar to an advent calendar. It represented the ninety days left until our wedding. Each day when Larry removed one piece of colored paper, it revealed the number of days left until our wedding. He sweetly complied with my creative effort, which was a good sign for our future, because he got many, many other opportunities to do that during our marriage. Some of my undertakings were actually well done, and others not so much.

Beautiful pink poinsettias were the flowers I chose to compliment the pink and red colors of the bouquets and four bridesmaids' dresses (which his mother had lovingly sewn). At that time, you were expected to open your wedding gifts in front of your guests. I still remember the thrill of seeing Mr. and Mrs. Larry Cornelius for the first time on one of the cards. I cherish the few wedding gifts I still have. One of them is a painting depicting an autumn scene of a beautiful coun-try landscape with a long, narrow creek. It was very special to me because the artist was one of my parents' friends, and she painted it just for us. This treasured keepsake has been in every home we had and is in the one where I now live alone.

Throughout the years, whenever anyone asked how many years we had been married, I would smile, give the answer, and then say, "It is day by day!" There were never any "deal breakers" between us, but we occasionally had misunderstandings. A long successful marriage is like a tapestry of different fabric, colors, texture, and thread. Looking at it you may make the observation of how naturally all of it seems to fit together, but turning it over you will find a few broken, tangled knots. That is how you know much work it took to create the final product. Happy marriages are worth all the effort it takes to work through the difficult times, and love has the amazing power to cover challenging situations between two people. We both became better people because we faced adversity together.

Each day of our lives together was recorded in a book only visible to God, and His unmistakable "ink" can be found on every page. Larry and I shared many once in-a lifetime experiences which made indelible imprints in our spirits. We gave life to two children who married and produced eight grandchildren for us. Together we buried our parents, and I gave the eulogies for both of our mothers. We thrived professionally with him in veterinary medicine and me as a classroom teacher.

When I retired, I became an author of Christian books, and this is my fourth one. Larry edited my first three books, spending many hours attempting to enhance my story telling. He was accustomed to authoring medical books, and so his exposure to my style of writing was quite an adventure for him (and me)! We were definitely a great team, and those books would not have been published without his encouragement.

Upon his retirement, Larry became a performer and gave himself the stage name of "Johnny Crash." He chose this name to reflect a little humor and because he liked the music of Johnny Cash. Larry loved the country music of several artists and collected several cowboy hats to wear when he sang their songs. He also enjoyed singing some of Elvis's music, and when he sang Elvis' songs, he wore a black wig, white coat with sequins, and a long gold necklace (that was my contribution). Larry definitely showed a different personality than when he was a conservative-minded professor of veterinary medicine. He certainly shocked some of his veterinarian colleagues. One of them, upon hearing Larry sing for the first time, revealed his surprise by saying, "I was *gobsmacked!*"

A life-changing event inspired his singing career. At the

age of sixty he was baptized and joined the church we had attended for over twenty-five years. This came about after he attended a men's three-day spiritual walk lead by his brother, Phil. He later told me, "I have always had it in me to accept the Lord as my Savior." In addition to me praying for him all those years, many others spoke to the Lord on his behalf. God was listening, speaking to his tender heart.

A few months after this, Larry was invited to join our church choir and he declined, but later accepted. (I believed he was prayed into the choir!) He had been part of a trio when he attended college, but that had been forty years prior. At first, he struggled with the music and sadly said, "I just can't sing anymore. My voice is gone." Everything changed when he bought a karaoke machine and some background tracks. Soon he joyfully exclaimed, "My voice is coming back!" I believe God made this happen for Larry and for me. I will always celebrate seeing God do this!

Larry began recording some non-commercial CDs to share with family and friends. After a couple of years, some of our grandchildren made a very encouraging observation and said his voice was getting better and better. He began to do many performances for local organizations and church groups. His life as an entertainer lasted for about thirteen years until his health began to fail. The music he left behind is his testimony of how God touched his life in a miraculous way.

Our daughter Jennifer also has a beautiful voice and she became his singing partner on many occasions, and the videos of some of these performances now give both of us great comfort. I will always believe it was no coincidence that all of this transpired after Larry made a commitment to the Lord.

Another pleasure of Larry's was teasing everyone around him (that included our Boston terrier Muffin who was part of our family for thirteen years). Larry's brother Phil was born when Larry was twenty- three. When Phil became an adult, it became obvious that they definitely shared the same sense of humor. After their mother passed away, I went with the family to the funeral home to make arrangements and choose a casket. We were tearfully looking at the choices when Phil suddenly said, "Barb, why don't you get in one so we can see how it will look." We all broke out in laughter, and I could almost hear Vera Cornelius say, "Now Phil, you need to behave." I believe that our laughter in the midst of sorrow was enjoyed by her and other family members in heaven. Maybe even our living God enjoyed that moment. I like to think He did.

Larry really, really liked to tease, and when I did not laugh at his remarks, he would just say, "Barb, you just don't have a sense of humor!" On the other hand, I was always thrilled when I could make him laugh. When we laughed together, we both felt tremendous pleasure in seeing each other's face. This was certainly a beautiful expression of our love for each other.

The almost sixty years we had together seems like a long time to some, but not to me. Some of our days seemed long, but the years just flew by. The love Larry and I felt for each other makes it worth my now mourning the loss of "us" on earth. I miss him terribly. Someone once told me that the depth of your grief is equal to how deeply you loved that person. They were right.

In the midst of my sorrow, I am greatly comforted knowing that the time I had with Larry will always exist. Nothing can erase it. The memories of love, laughter, and joy are forever stored inside my spirit. All of that resonates with the life I now lead. Many things he lovingly said to me come back to mind and I enjoy *hearing* them all over again. This enormous gift of sixty years with a man I loved deeply, and who in return loved me the same way, will never lose it value. The Lord provided this treasure for me. Nothing can take it away. It is forever mine and mine only.

My grief from not being able to see Larry on this side of eternity is sheltered with gratitude and the assurance I will see him again. When Jesus died on the cross, he cancelled death as the final destination for Larry and me. He cancelled it for you and all believers. The greatest example of God making beauty from ashes is His defeat of death and exchanging it for our eternal life with Him.

Until I see my beloved Larry again, I will just practice loving him on this side of eternity with the Lord at my side. Larry is in my future waiting for me. All of your deceased loved ones who knew the Lord are waiting for you. They are not lost. We know exactly where they are.

Larry blessed many people with his voice.

2 Corinthians 1:4-5

He comforts us in all our troubles so that we can comfort others. When they are troubled, we will be able to give them the same comfort God has given us.

Psalm 56:8

"You keep track of all my sorrows. You have collected all my tears in your bottle. You have recorded each one in your book."

John 11:33-35

When Jesus saw her weeping, and the Jews who had come along with her also weeping, he was deeply moved in spirit and troubled. "Where have you laid him?" he asked. "Come and see, Lord," they replied. Jesus wept.

1 Corinthians 15:42-45

So will it be with the resurrection of the dead. The body that is sown is perishable, it is raised imperishable. It is sown in dishonor, it is raised in glory; It is sown in weakness, it is raised in power; it is sown a natural body, it is raised a spiritual body.

Chapter Eighteen
The Power of Grief Shared

When my husband Larry recently passed away, I began experiencing grief with a "texture and color" that was different from when I lost close friends, my brother, parents, and other loved ones. My immense sorrow came from loving him so deeply and missing the life we had together. I felt like half of me was gone. I asked myself, "Is my faith real and strong enough to carry me through this dark valley?"

I was blessed with a long marriage, but it was not long enough. It would have never been long enough. Death is a huge shock, even when you see it coming. You discover that it was never stored safely away in the future. It was supposed to be in a place that was far away from your present experience. You cannot prepare in advance for this kind of pain, and who would want to? It is when your loved one has died that you challenge your reality and say to yourself, "This cannot be happening." The "future" comes barging into the present, and it hurts so very deeply.

I do not suffer alone. I rely on the Holy Spirit to give me strength to bear my grief in a way that reflects my faith. I know Larry is totally alive with our heavenly Father and waiting for me. Still, I seek comfort for my aching heart. I find that some of my friends who have also lost husbands have words of encouragement for me. The empowerment to console others sometimes comes from having walked the same lonely path they are now experiencing. You never want this attribute, but you fervently desire for God to use your pain to help others. I believe this is one way God creates great beauty from the ashes of sorrow.

I recently met Mimi who sixteen years ago suffered the death of her only child. Her daughter Erin was only in her early twenties when an accident took her life. Mimi suffered total emotional devastation for ten years after her loss. She retreated to a life which was then devoid of any joy, and carried a burden that was weighing her down every waking moment. She believed relief would come only at her death. She says today, "I was stuck in my grief." However, when her husband's health began to fail, she became "unstuck."

Mimi became her husband's caregiver, and for five years she put his needs above hers. After his death, something miraculous happened. Instead of falling back into the helpless pit of grief she experienced after her daughter's death, she became a beacon of light for others. She felt inspired to uplift others who were carrying a heavy burden of grief. She knew what that felt like. She also recently elected to be a facilitator in a thirteen-week program for people who were grieving over the death of a loved one. She gently and tenderly brought those attending under her "protective wings." I was there to see it.

I will never forget the time I spent with Mimi and the other leaders in this class. God has anointed her to give others hope, and help them find a way to regain happiness. No, sorrow has not disappeared from her life, but she is allowing God to use her to be Jesus to others. Her pain has not been wasted. God is using it to wrap His arms around those who are weighted down with sorrow. She has a quiet but powerful presence about her that allows you to sense the Holy Spirit manifested in her. She has walked through a dark valley with the Lord and found light waiting for her at the end. She now shares her journey with others to give them hope. I find her to be one of the most inspiring people I have ever met. I am grateful for her.

My loss also becomes a gain as I draw closer to the Lord because of my emotional pain. I feel His presence in a way I had not experienced before Larry's death. Larry left too soon, and I just wasn't ready to say good-bye. I never would have been ready to say good-bye. Because of my Lord, the good-bye is not permanent.

A few months after I became a widow, a cousin who is like a sister to me also lost her husband. When she shared her anguish with me, her words were," I know you understand what I am feeling." So, there it was, my new power to console others who had lost their husbands. With every death of a loved one, God gives us the ability to help others in pain. God's soothing balm flows generously between the grieved and the comforter.

Whenever I read in God's Word about Jesus standing at the tomb of Lazarus, I feel like I am standing next to Him. Jesus wept when He stood there. Now I am beside Him and weep for my loss. Jesus knew he was going to raise Lazarus from the dead and He also knew Lazarus would someday die again. Yet, our Lord's anguish over seeing his friend in a tomb surely gripped His heart. He knew it was not supposed to be that way for any of God's children, and so He went to the cross to rescue us.

Death can no longer hold us. Larry will rise from the dead, and I will rise from my death. Your loved ones gone from this earth who belonged to Him will live again. We will all rise together in the presence of the Lord. The ashes of death will be transformed into everlasting life for us. The sight of this reunion will be of unparalleled beauty in the universe. Take solace. This is your future.

The supernatural force of God's spirit in us is magnified when we reach out to others. Tears of sorrow comprise a universal language which needs no translation, just a response from a compassionate heart. God is intimately aware of our pain and King David in Psalm 56 says God even collects our tears in bottles. Our Heavenly Father knows how we feel and He offers Himself as the Supreme Comforter of the universe.

God rescued us with the death of His Only Son on the cross. He loved us so much that He paid the price to save us from death and replace it with eternal life. When our consoling arms and spirits reach out for others, we share the profound love that Jesus has for us. His brilliant light then comes spilling out and replaces the darkness. It is then that God's design of making beauty from ashes is there for the world to see! Praise Him!

Love you forever, Larry

Erin Tarpley

Loved Forever

Barbara J. Cornelius

<u>Deuteronomy 1:30-31</u>

There you saw how the LORD your God carried you, as a father carries his son, all the way you went until you reached this place.

<u>Isaiah 40:11</u>

He tends his flock like a shepherd: He gathers the lambs in his arms and carries them close to his heart; He gently leads those that have young.

Chapter Nineteen

A Tapestry of Miracles

It promised to be a sad Mother's Day for me, since it was my first one without my husband. Yet, I heard the encouraging words of a song echoing throughout the church sanctuary, "I will carry you through your darkest night when you are terrified. I will carry you when the waters rise. When your hope runs dry, I will carry you." These lyrics from the song "I Will Carry You" were being sung by my eldest grandson Brandon, and my daughter Jennifer on Mothers' Day in 2023. Their duet was a surprise gift for me and a blessing for the entire congregation. Jennifer had chosen it to commemorate her and her father's singing it fifteen years ago on Mother's Day in 2008. Jennifer and Brandon stood in the same place at the front of the sanctuary as she and her father had stood all those years ago. It was a God-given miracle then and it was also one now.

My husband Larry had a beautiful voice. I loved hearing it the first time I heard it in 1963 when he called to ask for a date; I loved hearing it during the last days of his life when it was difficult for him to speak. Whether it was in my presence, on the phone, or of a recording of his music, I never stopped enjoying his melodic voice. He came from a family who enjoyed music. In college he happened to meet two other male students who wanted to form a trio. These three young men sang for small audiences across the campus of Purdue University, and although it was just a hobby, it became the highlight of their college experience.

On one occasion before we were married, Larry sent me a cassette tape of a couple of their songs, and I loved hearing them so much I played the tape over and over. Unfortunately, at some point the tape disappeared so I no longer had any opportunities to enjoy it. A year after we were married, Larry and his friends graduated and went their separate ways. With the trio no longer together, Larry just stopped singing. Not meeting others who also liked to sing, and his need to focus on his career caused him to lose interest.

As the years passed, I yearned to hear him sing again. Sometimes I would stand next to him at church and strain to hear him as he softly sang with the congregation. In his retirement he became interested in music again, and I was thrilled. I frequently told him that I loved hearing his voice over any professional singer's. That was the absolute truth. He was so very talented. He once told a friend he had always wanted to find the ultimate gift for me, and it pleased him so much that his vocal talent seemed to fit the criteria.

His singing career before an audience began at our church in 2008. After many months of practicing at home, he asked our daughter Jennifer to sing a duet with him on Mother's Day. It took a lot of courage on Larry's part, because it had been over forty years since he last sung in public. It went beautifully. Later he confided in me that for a few moments before the music began, his mind went blank. He said that if Jennifer had not been standing next to him, it might have been a disaster!

Larry dedicated the song to his mother, on what turned out to be her last Mother's Day, and to a friend of ours whose husband had just died. A few months later, Larry sang his first solo at two of the church services. This led to his singing at senior citizen meetings, nursing homes, funerals, and even *a cappella* at graveside services. The Lord had given him a ministry of music and he relished using it with every opportunity that came his way. After a couple of years, our grandson Brandon who was twelve at the time, remarked, "Peepaw's voice is getting better and better."

The tape I lost all those years ago had by now been replaced with the non-commercial CDs he made using the background tracks of Elvis, Johnny Cash, Jim Reeves, and several country music stars. Larry also recorded some CDs of several Christian songs which I treasure even more fiercely now that he is gone. One of those is the duet "I Will Carry You" that Jennifer and he sang in 2008. Today, every time I play one of his CDs, I relive the elation of being with him and hearing him sing. The grief of missing him I carry today is lightened when I can hear a recording of his voice. I am so grateful God provided that for me.

This very reserved man became much more outgoing when he sang. His new confidence released him to use the talent God had given him decades ago. I feel certain that his gift was meant to glorify the Lord and bless many others. I have made copies of some of his recordings for the grandchildren, and perhaps they will someday play his songs for their children. No amount of monetary inheritance could possibly be more valuable than the music he left behind.

Larry would have been bursting with pride this last Mother's Day when his eldest grandson and daughter sang. Hearing the duet in 2008 was a very nice surprise, and the one sung Mother's Day 2023 will always be treasured by me.

Brandon was a premature baby and almost passed away five times the day he was born. Today he is very healthy and stands over six feet tall. He had not sung in front of a group since he was twelve years old, and he soon will be twenty-six. Brandon's whole life has been a miracle, and his confidence to sing publicly after so many years demonstrates the courage his grandfather modeled for him.

Jennifer has also had close calls with death, and God has preserved her life to glorify Him with her music. She has her father's talent to inspire others with her voice. She also has his courage to put her nervousness aside to use her gift and claim her calling from the Lord. I am sure that both she and Brandon make God smile when they sing.

Larry's, Jennifer's and Brandon's voices have been given by the Lord to weave a family tapestry of miracles. All three of them glorify Him with their music. Although Larry now sings with the angels, I feel that he was present on this last Mother's Day. The Lord took the sadness of his no longer being at my side, and wrapped it into a beautiful reminiscence. He turned my ashes into a beautiful new memory.

What have you been called to do that seems beyond your courage? It does not depend on you only. It depends on your willingness to step forward, and God will then take you the rest of the way.

He will walk through the "fire" carrying you in His arms, and the ashes of your anxiety, lack of confidence, low self-worth, sorrow, and desperation will be no more. The beautiful, glorious transformation that makes you a new creation will exist for all of eternity. The testimony you leave behind will be the greatest legacy of wealth you could ever give your descendants.

You are not alone.

The Lord will carry you through any tribulation that comes your way. He will carry you through your darkest night when you are terrified.

Psalm 40:3

He put a new song in my mouth, a hymn of praise to our God. Many will see and fear the Lord and put their trust in him.

Psalm 144:9

I will sing a new song to you, O God! I will sing your praises with a ten-stringed harp.

Psalm 96:1-2

Sing a new song to the Lord! Sing it everywhere around the world! Sing out his praises! Bless his name. Each day tell someone that he saves.

Chapter Twenty

God Fills Our Lives with Breathtaking Music

The audience of a few thousand people seemed to collectively hold its breath as the petite twelve-year-old girl nervously pondered the question posed to her. She had chosen an ambitious Aretha Franklin song for her audition in front of the four judges. Her performance was being taped and would be shown at a future date to millions of people. This very brave child had just been stopped by one of the judges in the middle of her song. He told her the track she was using was dreadful, and asked her if she could sing it again a cappella. Whoa!

As she tearfully absorbed the shock of his request, she was offered a large cup of water by the same judge. He placed it into her quivering hands as the tears cascaded down her cheeks. She then looked to the wings where her nervous parents were standing. Smiling, she said in a very sweet southern accent, "Well, *that* just happened!" Her gift of humor in the midst of a nerve-wracking situation revealed how she was coping with her situation, and this made everyone in the audience smile as they glimpsed the mettle of this child.

Her reaction extended grace to the rude judge and everyone present by revealing the lens through which she viewed the world. The out-going joyful nature she had exhibited when talking with the judges before she sang had already given her great favor with the audience. Seeing her response under tremendous pressure only increased the motivation of the audience to cheer her on. She had completely won them over.

When she sang the song a second time without the distraction of the low-quality track, her beautiful voice shined through as she navigated the three key changes in the song. She gave a brilliant and courageous performance that would have been stunning for a talented adult, but for this young girl to do it was absolutely thrilling! At the conclusion of her song, the judges and the audience stood and cheered at the top of their lungs. The intensity of this rousing response had perhaps been increased by the gallant way in which she had dealt with adversity. Adversity is not always the enemy. It certainly was true in this situation.

Watching the audition video and reflecting about the inspiring lesson this young girl gave the world prompted me to remember myself at the age of twelve when I was in the sixth grade. I looked nothing like this child. I looked like an adult. I was five feet six inches tall and weighed one hundred and forty pounds. My mother was afraid that I was going to be a giant! Fortunately, I stopped growing in both height and weight that year.

Despite my lack of confidence about my personal appearance, I decided to write a play for my 6th grade group project in language arts. I suffered a big hit to my self-esteem when my group rejected my finished product. They dashed my spirits by telling me, "We don't think you know what you are doing." They were probably not wrong, but when I look back at this memory, I am astounded that I even had the nerve to attempt writing a play. Somehow their rejection planted seeds of defiance which motivated me in my future aspirations. I don't like to be told I am not capable of doing something I want to do. I am pretty sure my classmates from so very long ago would be dumbfounded if they knew that in the last few years, I have authored four books.

Another life-defining situation occurred the next year when I was in seventh grade. My social studies teacher told my father that he didn't know if I was college material. My father who knew me well, repeated his comment to me. It hurt to hear those words, but they made me angry—very angry. I decided I would prove my social studies teacher wrong, so I started spending many more hours on my school work. Many years later I had a great desire to tell that teacher I earned three college degrees. I was not able to locate him, but in all honesty, he gave me a great gift with his words.

I wrote a poem when I was twelve expressing the anguish I felt and would feel for many years. It was entitled: "Why am I here?" I desperately wanted God to reveal His purpose for me on this earth. My nine year-old brother, who had been three years older than me, had died, but here I was still living. I thought the wrong child had died. Why was I still here? I didn't understand until decades later that God had a different plan for my life. The wrong child had not died, it was just that my story was meant to be told through a long life. God had not made a mistake in keeping me alive. He wanted my individual, unique story to be completed.

Looking back at myself all those years ago, I see a young girl carrying an enormous amount of emotional pain. She couldn't know that God was giving her a storehouse of words to benefit her in the different seasons of her life. Nothing she experienced would be wasted. All of it would be used to see God's plan for her life after she was able to stop focusing on distracting, negative messages. God had given her a special *song* for her life. No one else had her *song*.

The inferior background track, muting the beautiful voice of the talented child in the talent competition, simulated the kind of destructive, background noises we hear throughout our lives. They hinder us from recognizing our God given talents and tempt us to focus instead on the critical comments of others. I have heard those soul-depleting sounds throughout my life.

This noise begins early on for everyone. You hear many words of negativity and doubt your self-worth. Many, many accomplished people throughout history have had the same challenges and were exposed to the deafening sounds of discouragement. Yet, they were able to discount the *noise* and rise up to be who God meant them to be. The Old Testament is full of stories of God's anointed facing great adversity and yet ascending above it to claim the calling on their lives.

Check out the story of Joseph in the Old Testament. He faced a tremendous amount of adversity in his life. When he was seventeen, his jealous brothers threw him into a pit and then sold him as a slave. He eventually obtained a position as a distinguished servant in a household in Egypt. Later, adversity again came to him when the wife of his master accused him of attempted rape. He was then thrown into a dark, menacing prison, and that just happened to be a part of God's plan for him.

A few years went by and Joseph's circumstances changed. He had now been seasoned by all that has happened to him, and he had become a mature leader unmatched by anyone around him. Then, something unexpected happened. His God-given ability to interpret a dream for Pharaoh led him to be released from prison and he became second in command to him. Thirty years after their betrayal, his brothers came to Egypt to save their family from starvation and the brother they threw away became the one to save them and forgive them. Joseph found a way to walk in faith with God and draw a deaf ear to all the distracting, disconcerting things that came his way. He found the *song* that could only be sung by him. His story has now been told for a few thousand years and inspired millions of people.

Another heartening story in the Old Testament is that of King David. Like Joseph, his brothers challenged him. They taunted him when he said that he was going to defend Israel against the ten-foot-tall Goliath. They saw their brother as merely a young shepherd boy with no real-life experiences and certainly none at the battle front. Their assessment of him was that he was an immature teenager who had no idea how ludicrous his decision was to face Goliath with just five stones and a sling shot.

David however, driven by his devotion to God, stood his ground declaring that no giant on his watch was going to get by with defaming the living God. David was victorious for God that day and every time someone tells his story or reads about it in the Bible, David is again victorious for God.

Later, we see that after this incident, David played the lyre for King Saul to soothe his troubled spirit. David used this instrument to express the music he heard inside himself, and Saul was always the better for hearing it. Today when we read the Psalms in the Old Testament which were written by King David, we can "hear" his music. His inspired words have blessed millions of people for a few thousand years. They encourage us to hear the "melody" God puts in the midst of our life's struggles and challenges. This in turn emboldens us to cancel out the intrusion of all the dissonance and sing our **song**. The world needs to hear it.

Everyone has their own individual song to sing to the world. Our awesome Heavenly Father is always creating opportunities for us to find our song in the midst of a world full of diversions. He uses adversity as well as affirmation to shape us into a one-of a-kind person for His kingdom. Sometimes it is early in our lives when we recognize His Hand on us, and for others it is much later. During all that time He is making something beautiful from our ashes.

Every day God is encouraging us to hear the music He placed inside of us. Give a deaf ear to the dissonance around you and sing loudly and beautifully the song God has written for your life. He gave it to you before you took your first breath. No one else has your song. Let the world hear it.

Why Am I Here?

Father, tell me why am I here.

Why is there so much sickness?

And why so much fear?

Please, why am I here?

Father, why is there so much sadness

And why so many a tear?

Please tell me why I am here.

Father, will I faithfully follow Thee

And fully for Thy cause will I plea?

Or will I be just another lost, not really ever free?

Father, let me tell others why we are here

And how they can release their darkest fears.

Let me share the music you gave to me, forgetting my tears

And through Your Son, find the reason you put us here.

Father, I sing praises to You throughout eternity!

Epilogue

I Had a Good Time

Here I am in the fourth quarter of my life and I am in a full sprint. I can't see how much time is left on the clock, and I am grateful about that. My sweet husband left ahead of me, and I am sure he is waiting for me. I am totally amazed our sixty years together went so quickly. I was a young woman not so long ago, and yet here I am, not just a senior citizen with new, wonderful discounts, but an elderly woman in her 70s. If only the mirrors in my house accommodated my illusion of youth, I would not have to acknowledge reality. Maybe mirrors are not my only barrier to the truth, but I like thinking that way.

Still, my grateful heart yearns to tell God, "I had a good time." No, tragedy did not escape me. No, gut-wrenching trials did not avoid me. No, fame and fortune did not find me. I just loved experiencing the presence of God in all that came. Just as a forest fire produces ashes which release nutrients back into the soil, I saw God touch my "ashes" to release beauty into my life. Sometimes I recognized this happening quickly, and then there were times when it took a very long while for me see it. Yet I always knew to look for it.

He comforts and walks beside me in every trial, even when whining is all I manage to do. Many times, when overwhelming weariness comes, He carries me in His arms. I feel confident that the prayers of others help to make this happen. I'm pretty sure when joy suddenly appears, He laughs and even dances with me.

Some of my goofiness and clumsiness surely tickles His giant funny bone. I often say, "God would fix me, but He is just having too good of a time watching me." At least that is my theory about why I haven't become a more coordinated and functioning adult lady. I surmise that He will clarify this issue when I get my "promotion" and permanently reside with Him.

I have felt God's love in special ways when I walked through many rough patches. This happened when He gave me great comfort through His Word, sent others to encourage me, and let me witness some of His miraculous answers to prayers. His beauty always arose from the ashes.

I learned to talk to God with great intensity when I was four years old and my brother Bobby was seriously ill. When he died three years later, I told God He had chosen the wrong child to live. Over the long years of my life, He took my sense of unworthiness to teach me about His grace and let me realize the great value I have in Him. He loves me "best", and He loves all His children "best." I love being a favored child, don't you!

When I was twenty-two, I had a terrifying car accident caused by a wheel suddenly coming off my car. At the time I was traveling fifty-five miles an hour on a very busy highway, and at one point I was headed toward a deep ravine. The car then came to a sudden stop at a right angle to the road. I miraculously escaped unharmed. I came to believe God sent His messengers to save me that day. After one of my most beloved childhood friends died a few months later in a car accident, He taught me to trust Him about my survival and her not having the same miracle. He has kept her memory vividly lodged in my heart all my life, and I know I will see her again. Ann and I will again sit quietly in a place of serenity and enjoy each other's company. Perhaps we will share a few giggles as we marvel over the happiness of being with God.

All during my thirty plus years as a classroom teacher, God came into my space and taught me how to laugh, learn, and surrender my struggles to Him. My occupation gave me a front row seat where I could see Him touch children with His presence. So many precious souls were entrusted to me, and I prayed for Him to be divinely present in all that took place. It is my solace that even though mistakes were surely made by me, God as the "master storyteller" used them to weave blessings into their life stories.

My own two children grew into adulthood at what seemed to be a rapid pace, married wonderful people, and gave me eight grandchildren. I intentionally try to savor the time I have with them, and yet it passes quickly like sand through a funnel in a bottle. The older I get, the faster it passes. I smile as I know that this is the goodness of life being experienced in God's fullness.

So much of my life was weighted down with insecurity and being self-consciousness but now I am almost giddy with seeing my life differently through the lens God has provided. This gift was there for me to receive all along, but I have only in these last few years chosen to accept it. I have been known to tell people that old age is a lot of fun! They respond with great skepticism, "That's not what I hear!"

No, the physical ailments that accompany aging are not fun. However, the ability to laugh at yourself and see the possible humor in awkward situations is pure gold. When you are no longer spending so much time "inward focused", the opportunities for finding humor are unlimited.

When recently asked by a bank employee if I knew how to use the ATM machine, I said, "No. I am senile, but my granddaughter can teach me how to use it!" (The other people in line thought my comment was pretty funny.). Perhaps because an old face spoke these words, the teller responded with a great big smile! I just enjoy interacting with the people who hand me my money. Don't you? Some of my best conversations have been with total strangers who also had a sense of humor. Honestly, you can get by with more stuff when you are an old lady. Are you smiling as you read this? See what I mean.

Yes, I had a good time, Father. I am thankful for the time you gave me here on earth, and I am eternally grateful for the life waiting for me when I go home to be with you. In the meanwhile, I want to make you proud of me by telling Your story wherever I go.

Father, I am grateful that you took my sins, failures, and hurts that pierced my spirit and let me see you transform them into victories for my soul. Many times, I couldn't see your Hand move in the presence of my defeats, but now, I see evidence that you were always there. Thank you for turning so many of my ashes into something beautiful for Your kingdom.

I know that at the end of my story I will be awarded the greatest promotion possible for any human soul. Why did you think I was worth giving your Son's life to provide this for me? My limited human understanding cannot grasp the answer to that. Your grace overwhelms me. Your love set aside my unworthiness and replaced it with the reflection of You inside of me. I have loved the journey that made me look more like You. I yearn for my total transformation when all earthly burdens cease to exist and <u>all</u> my ashes are replaced with the beauty of You, the Living God.

Cornelius family

singing

marriage

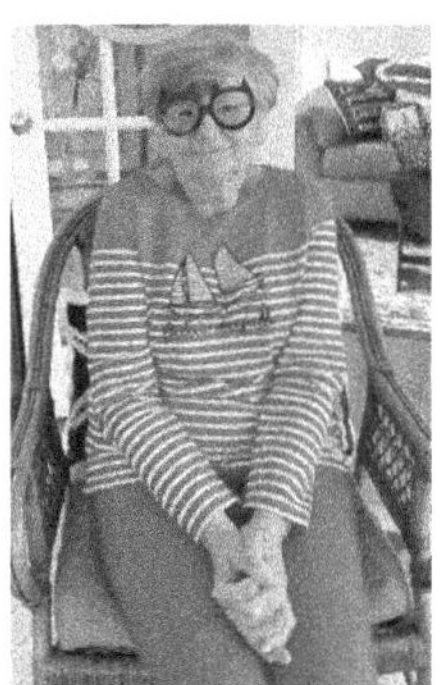

laughter

author

flying with my cousin Rick
Spencer, (Southwest Airlines)

lighthearted moments

fun times